Edward de Chazal

Ed Pegg

# in company 3.0

### STARTER STUDENT'S BOOK

# in company 3.0 at a glance

**10 Business communication units** focusing on current business issues and everyday skills for the workplace

- Learning objectives to track your progress
- Fluency and communication activities on every page

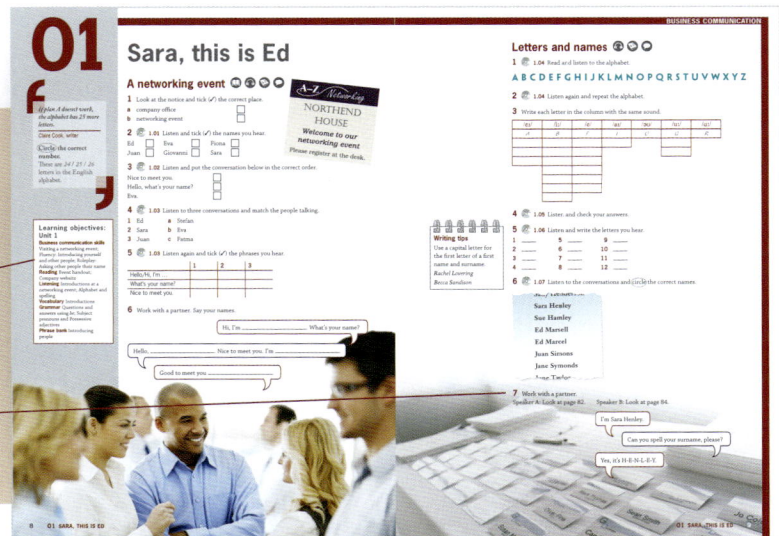

**5 Survival scenarios** offering challenging case studies that simulate business situations and allow interaction with the language in a dynamic way

- Engaging videos illustrate true-to-life scenarios

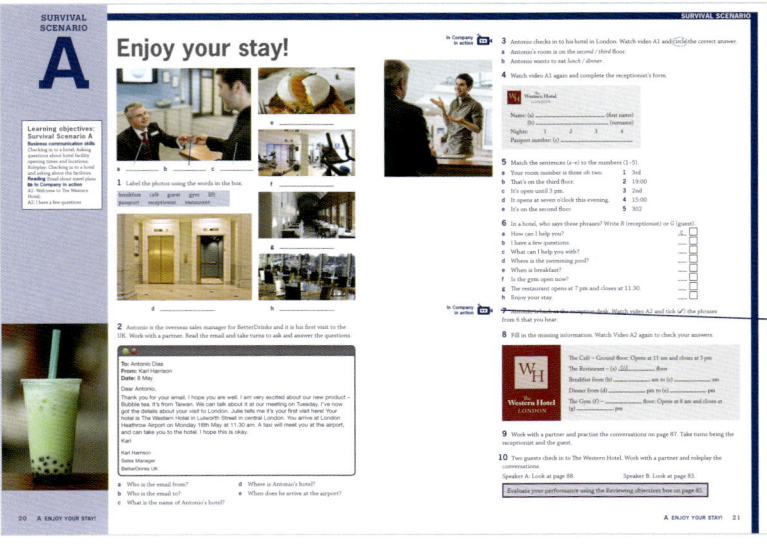

**10 Language links** consolidating grammar and extending vocabulary from the Business communication units

- Grammar reference with detailed explanations of key points
- Phrase bank of key take-away phrases for quick revision
- Evaluate your progress using the Reviewing objectives box
- Extra space to make notes as you study

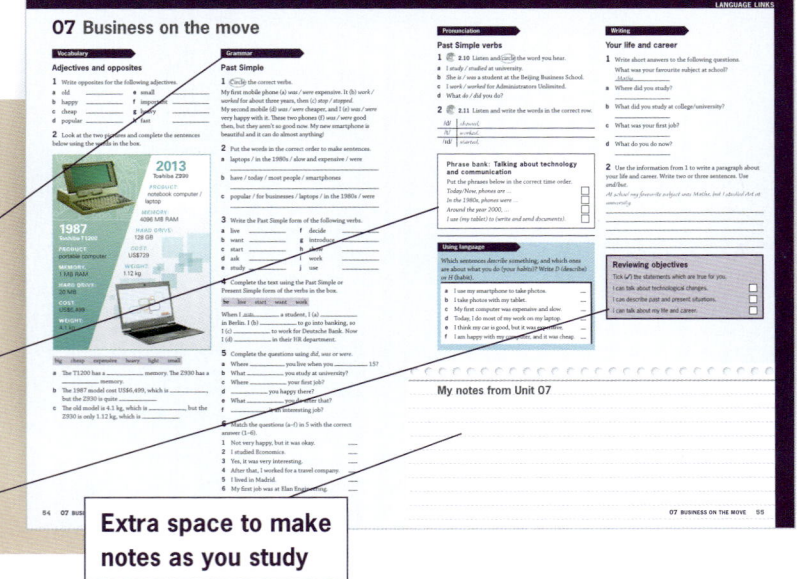

# INTRODUCTION

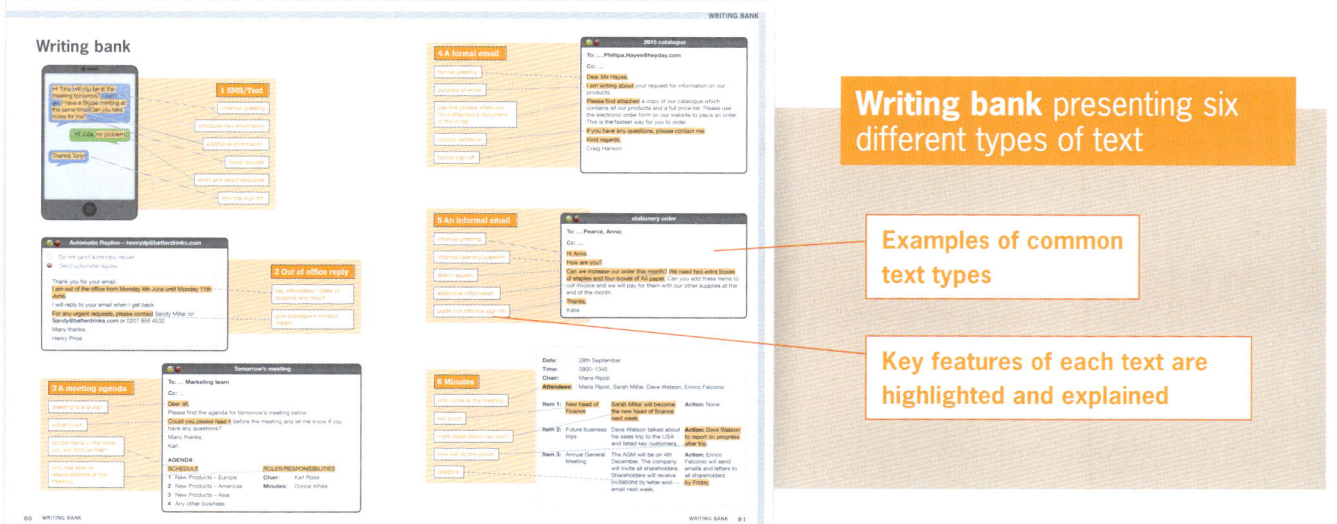

**Writing bank** presenting six different types of text

Examples of common text types

Key features of each text are highlighted and explained

## Extra material

- Irregular verb list
- Additional material for communicative activities
- Reviewing objectives statements for survival skills scenario activities
- Listening scripts

# Online Workbook and Student's Resource Centre

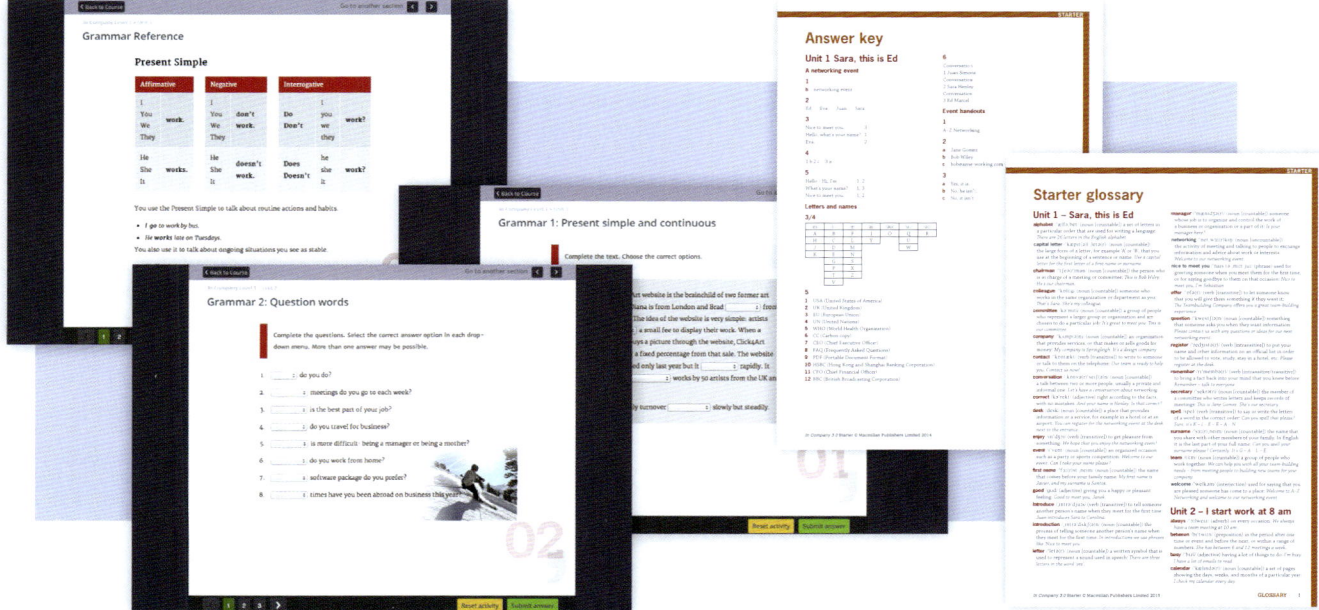

## Online Workbook

Everything you need to build and expand on the Student's Book material outside the classroom, and all accessible online:
- Interactive activities to practise:
  - Vocabulary
  - Grammar
  - Reading
  - Writing
  - Listening
- Automatic markbook
- Grammar reference
- Writing reference

## Student's Resource Centre

An extensive collection of resources, all available to download:
- Student's Book audio
- 'In Company in action' – Student's Book scenario videos
- 'In Company interviews' – additional video material
- Glossary
- Answer key
- Phrase banks

# Contents

Learner information p6

| Unit | Business communication skills | Reading and listening | Language links |
|---|---|---|---|
| **01** Sara, this is Ed p8 | Visiting a networking event **Fluency** Introducing yourself and other people **Roleplay** Asking other people their name | **Reading** Event handout Company website **Listening** Introductions at a networking event Alphabet and spelling | **Vocabulary** Introductions **Grammar** Questions and answers using *be* Subject pronouns Possessives adjectives **Phrase bank** Introducing people |
| **02** I start work at 8 am p14 | Using numbers and times Looking at work routines **Fluency** Talking about your daily work routine **In Company interviews** Units 1–2 | **Reading** Text messages Article about a typical day in the office **Listening** Conversations about daily routines | **Vocabulary** Numbers and work-related verbs **Grammar** Present Simple with key words for work Questions with *When*, *What time* and *How many* **Phrase bank** Telling the time |
| **Survival scenario A:** Enjoy your stay! p20 | Checking into a hotel Asking questions about hotel facility opening times and locations **Roleplay** Checking into a hotel and asking about the facilities | **Reading** Email about travel plans **In Company in action** A1: Welcome to The Western Hotel A2: I have a few questions | |
| **03** Where do you work? p22 | Looking at jobs and companies **Fluency** Talking about your job and your company | **Reading** Work the Net profiles **Listening** Conversations about jobs, sectors and companies | **Vocabulary** Jobs, sectors and numbers *10–100* (tens), *100–1,000* (hundreds), *10,000–50,000* (thousands) **Grammar** Questions with *do/does* **Phrase bank** Describing your job and company |
| **04** Can I help you? p28 | Making simple telephone calls Making arrangements **Roleplay** Leaving a message **Fluency** Talking about dates **In Company interviews** Units 3–4 | **Listening** Telephone calls to leave a message and to arrange a meeting | **Vocabulary** Telephone numbers Dates, days and months **Grammar** *Can* for requests and possibility **Phrase bank** Telephone phrases |
| **Survival scenario B:** It's very close p34 | Saying where places are in a town Saying where places are in an office **Roleplay** Asking where places are in a town | **Reading** Text message about plans to meet **In Company in action** B1: I want to get to the office B2: Go straight to the meeting room | |
| **05** I'm here to see Jo p36 | Making small talk **Roleplay** Visiting an office | **Reading** Emails Office floor plans **Listening** Conversations with small talk Showing someone around the office | **Vocabulary** Small talk Job titles Departments **Grammar** Prepositions: *in*, *on*, *opposite*, *next to* **Phrase bank** Arranging a visit Visiting a company |

# CONTENTS

| Unit | Business communication skills | Reading and listening | Language links |
|---|---|---|---|
| **06** **Let's make a start** p42 | Taking part in meetings **Fluency** Discussing types of advertising **In Company interviews** Units 5–6 | **Reading** Meeting agenda Blog post **Listening** Introduction to a meeting Conversation about meetings Marketing meeting | **Vocabulary** Meeting words and phrases **Grammar** Frequency words, verbs, nouns and time phrases Questions with *How often/Do you* **Phrase bank** Useful phrases for meetings |
| **Survival scenario C:** **Don't mention it** p48 | Asking for a favour Responding to requests for a favour **Roleplay** Making and responding to requests for a favour | **Reading** Business article: How to ask for a favour **In Company in action** C1: I know you're busy but … C2: There's just one more thing | |
| **07** **Business on the move** p50 | Talking about changes in technology **Fluency** Talking about your life and career | **Reading** Article about changing technology **Listening** The life of a business speaker *-ed* pronunciation | **Vocabulary** Adjectives and opposites **Grammar** Past Simple **Phrase bank** Talking about technology and communication |
| **08** **I'd like to talk about …** p56 | Giving presentations **Fluency** Talking about changes and results **Roleplay** Giving a sales presentation **In Company interviews** Units 7–8 | **Reading** Email about investment opportunities **Listening** Presentation about sales results Question and answer session | **Vocabulary** Describing change **Grammar** Past Simple irregular verbs Questions and negatives in the past **Phrase bank** Useful presentation language |
| **Survival scenario D:** **Click the icon** p62 | Giving instructions and responding to instructions for common office tasks **Roleplay** Giving instructions for sending an email and printing a document | **Reading** Email about a training session **In Company in action** D1: It's really easy, I promise D2: For an outside line, press 9 | |
| **09** **Where should I stay?** p64 | Planning a business event **Roleplay** Organizing food for a business event **Fluency** Giving travel tips to visitors | **Reading** Business invitation **Listening** Planning business events Talking about places | **Vocabulary** Opposites Food Places **Grammar** Making suggestions *some* and *any* **Phrase bank** Asking for suggestions |
| **10** **Is cash okay?** p70 | Negotiating **Roleplay** Negotiating a deal **In Company interviews** Units 9–10 | **Reading** Email about a negotiation Contract **Listening** Negotiations about delivery, price and discounts | **Vocabulary** Contract language **Grammar** Talking about the future **Phrase bank** Requesting, refusing and accepting |
| **Survival scenario E:** **What's Eton mess?** p76 | Describing food Talking about food from different countries **Fluency** Describing a dish from your country or region | **Reading** Menu of a British restaurant **In Company in action** E1: How about a British restaurant? E2: Tell us about Spanish food | |

Irregular verb list p78    Writing bank p80    Additional material p82    Listening scripts p89

# Learner information

## Icons

The icons show the skills you will practise in each section of the Student's Book.

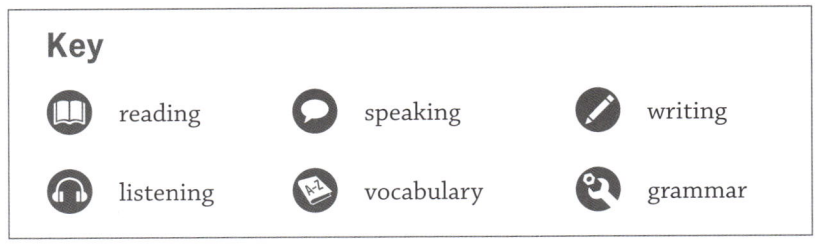

**Skills practised in this section**

**Reading activities 1, 2, 3**

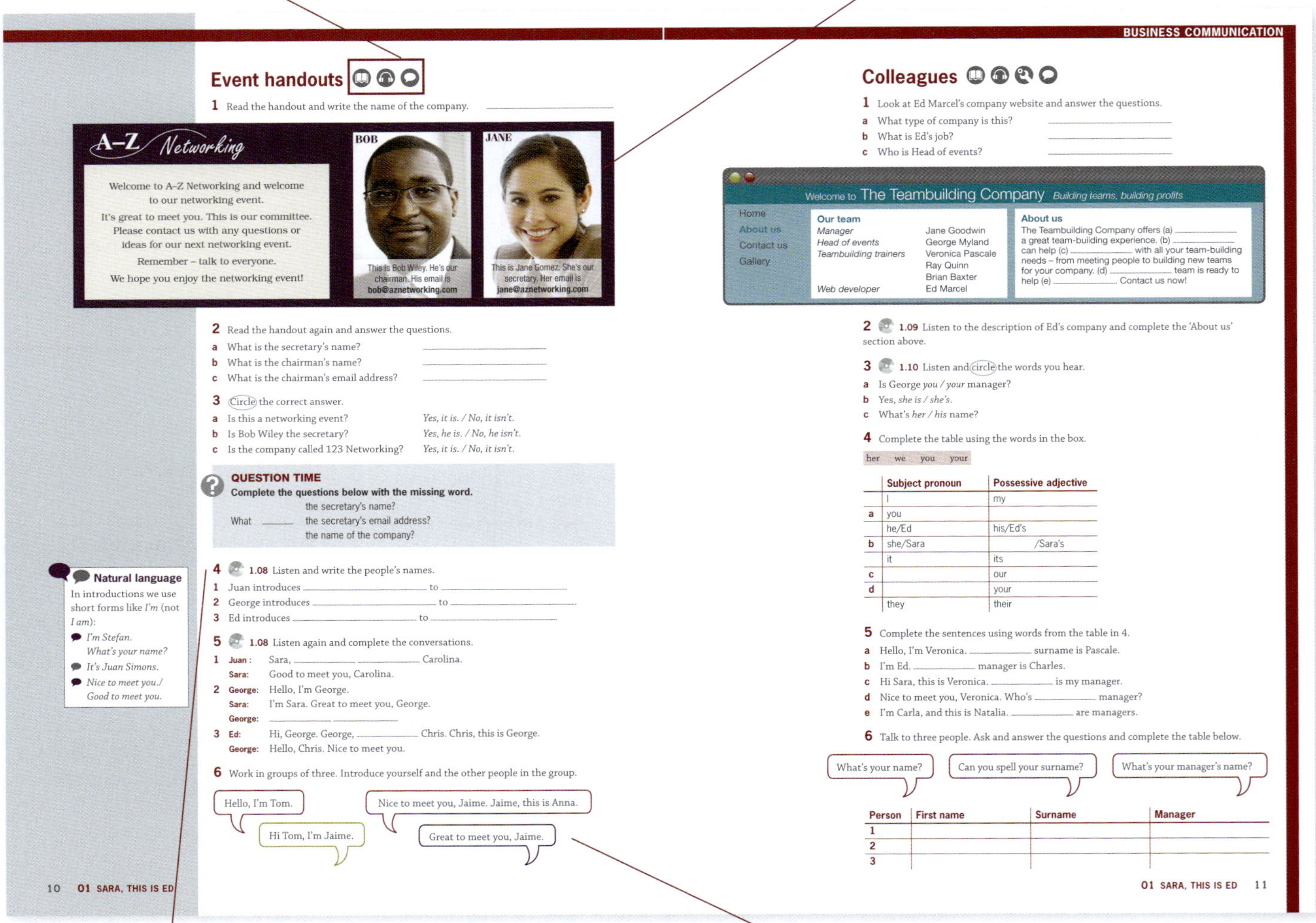

**Listening activities 4, 5**

**Speaking activity 6**

# in company 3.0 Student's Book instructions

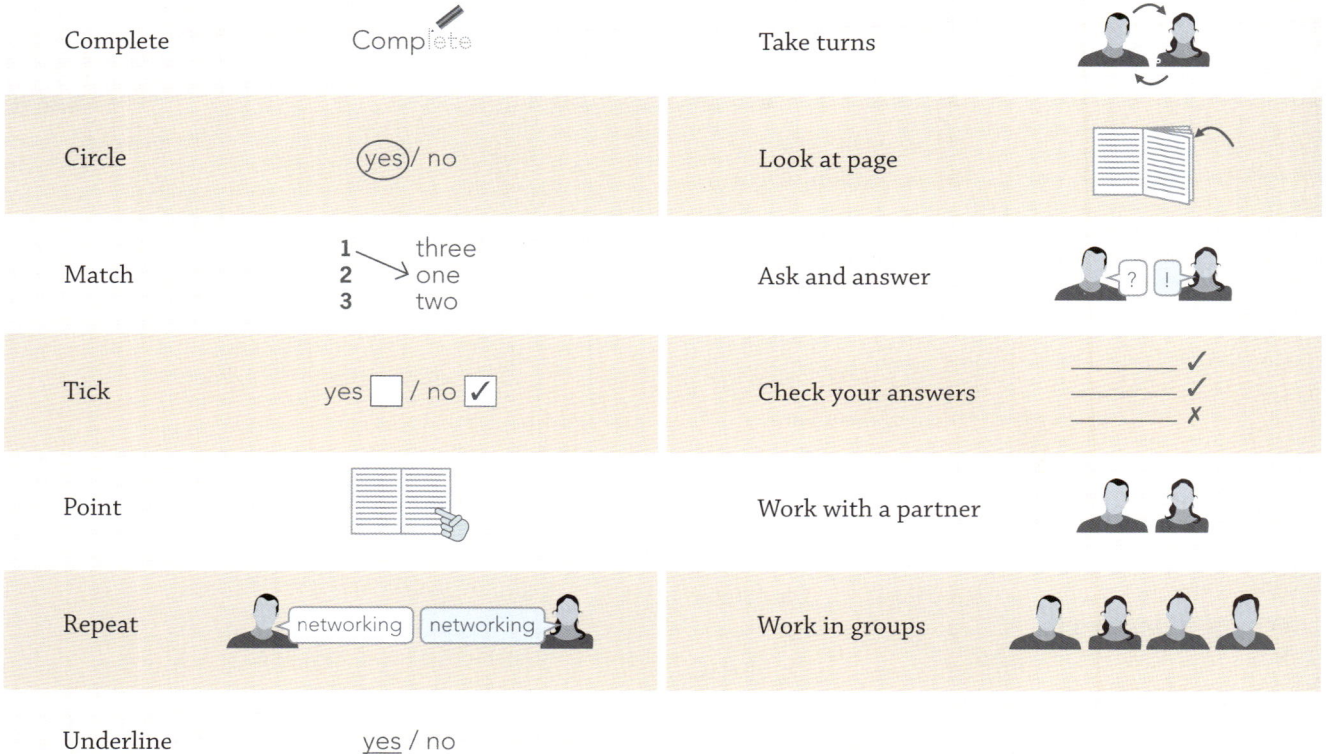

## Classroom language

Try to use English all the time in class. Here are some useful expressions.

# 01

*If plan A doesn't work, the alphabet has 25 more letters.*

Claire Cook, writer

Circle the correct number.
There are 24 / 25 / 26 letters in the English alphabet.

**Learning objectives: Unit 1**
**Business communication skills** Visiting a networking event; Fluency: Introducing yourself and other people; Roleplay: Asking other people their name
**Reading** Event handout; Company website
**Listening** Introductions at a networking event; Alphabet and spelling
**Vocabulary** Introductions
**Grammar** Questions and answers using *be*; Subject pronouns and Possessive adjectives
**Phrase bank** Introducing people

# Sara, this is Ed

## A networking event

**A–Z Networking**
**NORTHEND HOUSE**
Welcome to our networking event
Please register at the desk.

**1** Look at the notice and tick (✓) the correct place.
a company office ☐
b networking event ☐

**2** 🔊 1.01 Listen and tick (✓) the names you hear.
Ed ☐   Eva ☐   Fiona ☐
Juan ☐   Giovanni ☐   Sara ☐

**3** 🔊 1.02 Listen and put the conversation below in the correct order.
Nice to meet you. ☐
Hello, what's your name? ☐
Eva. ☐

**4** 🔊 1.03 Listen to three conversations and match the people talking.
1 Ed        a Stefan
2 Sara      b Eva
3 Juan      c Fatma

**5** 🔊 1.03 Listen again and tick (✓) the phrases you hear.

|  | 1 | 2 | 3 |
|---|---|---|---|
| Hello/Hi, I'm … |  |  |  |
| What's your name? |  |  |  |
| Nice to meet you. |  |  |  |

**6** Work with a partner. Say your names.

Hi, I'm _____. What's your name?

Hello, _____. Nice to meet you. I'm _____.

Good to meet you _____.

**BUSINESS COMMUNICATION**

## Letters and names

**1** 🎧 **1.04** Read and listen to the alphabet.

**A B C D E F G H I J K L M N O P Q R S T U V W X Y Z**

**2** 🎧 **1.04** Listen again and repeat the alphabet.

**3** Write each letter in the column with the same sound.

| /eɪ/ | /iː/ | /e/ | /aɪ/ | /əʊ/ | /uː/ | /ɑː/ |
|------|------|-----|------|------|------|------|
| A    | B    | F   | I    | O    | Q    | R    |
|      |      |     |      |      |      |      |
|      |      |     |      |      |      |      |
|      |      |     |      |      |      |      |
|      |      |     |      |      |      |      |
|      |      |     |      |      |      |      |
|      |      |     |      |      |      |      |

**4** 🎧 **1.05** Listen and check your answers.

**5** 🎧 **1.06** Listen and write the letters you hear.

1 ____    5 ____    9 ____
2 ____    6 ____    10 ____
3 ____    7 ____    11 ____
4 ____    8 ____    12 ____

**Writing tips**
Use a capital letter for the first letter of a first name and surname.
*Rachel Lovering*
*Becca Sandison*

**6** 🎧 **1.07** Listen to the conversations and (circle) the correct names.

Sally Henderson
Sara Henley
Sue Hamley
Ed Marsell
Ed Marcel
Juan Simons
Jane Symonds
June Taylor

**7** Work with a partner.
Speaker A: Look at page 82.    Speaker B: Look at page 84.

I'm Sara Henley.

Can you spell your surname, please?

Yes, it's H-E-N-L-E-Y.

**01 SARA, THIS IS ED**

## Event handouts

**1** Read the handout and write the name of the company. _____

### A–Z Networking

Welcome to A–Z Networking and welcome to our networking event.

It's great to meet you. This is our committee. Please contact us with any questions or ideas for our next networking event.

Remember – talk to everyone.

We hope you enjoy the networking event!

BOB

This is Bob Wiley. He's our chairman. His email is bob@aznetworking.com

JANE

This is Jane Gomez. She's our secretary. Her email is jane@aznetworking.com

**2** Read the handout again and answer the questions.
a What is the secretary's name? _____
b What is the chairman's name? _____
c What is the chairman's email address? _____

**3** Circle the correct answer.
a Is this a networking event? Yes, it is. / No, it isn't.
b Is Bob Wiley the secretary? Yes, he is. / No, he isn't.
c Is the company called 123 Networking? Yes, it is. / No, it isn't.

### QUESTION TIME
**Complete the questions below with the missing word.**

What _____ the secretary's name?
         the secretary's email address?
         the name of the company?

 **Natural language**

In introductions we use short forms like *I'm* (not *I am*):

- *I'm Stefan. What's your name?*
- *It's Juan Simons.*
- *Nice to meet you./ Good to meet you.*

**4** 1.08 Listen and write the people's names.
1 Juan introduces _____ to _____.
2 George introduces _____ to _____.
3 Ed introduces _____ to _____.

**5** 1.08 Listen again and complete the conversations.
1 **Juan:** Sara, _____ _____ Carolina.
   **Sara:** Good to meet you, Carolina.
2 **George:** Hello, I'm George.
   **Sara:** I'm Sara. Great to meet you, George.
   **George:** _____ _____.
3 **Ed:** Hi, George. George, _____ Chris. Chris, this is George.
   **George:** Hello, Chris. Nice to meet you.

**6** Work in groups of three. Introduce yourself and the other people in the group.

Hello, I'm Tom.

Hi Tom, I'm Jaime.

Nice to meet you, Jaime. Jaime, this is Anna.

Great to meet you, Jaime.

## BUSINESS COMMUNICATION

## Colleagues

**1** Look at Ed Marcel's company website and answer the questions.

a What type of company is this?  _____
b What is Ed's job?  _____
c Who is Head of events?  _____

---

**Welcome to The Teambuilding Company**  *Building teams, building profits*

Home
**About us**
Contact us
Gallery

**Our team**
Manager — Jane Goodwin
Head of events — George Myland
Teambuilding trainers — Veronica Pascale
Ray Quinn
Brian Baxter
Web developer — Ed Marcel

**About us**
The Teambuilding Company offers (a) _____ a great team-building experience. (b) _____ can help (c) _____ with all your team-building needs – from meeting people to building new teams for your company. (d) _____ team is ready to help (e) _____. Contact us now!

---

**2** 1.09 Listen to the description of Ed's company and complete the 'About us' section above.

**3** 1.10 Listen and (circle) the words you hear.

a Is George *you / your* manager?
b Yes, *she is / she's*.
c What's *her / his* name?

**4** Complete the table using the words in the box.

her    we    you    your

|   | Subject pronoun | Possessive adjective |
|---|---|---|
|   | I | my |
| a | you |  |
|   | he/Ed | his/Ed's |
| b | she/Sara | _____ /Sara's |
|   | it | its |
| c |  | our |
| d |  | your |
|   | they | their |

**5** Complete the sentences using words from the table in 4.

a Hello, I'm Veronica. _____ surname is Pascale.
b I'm Ed. _____ manager is Charles.
c Hi Sara, this is Veronica. _____ is my manager.
d Nice to meet you, Veronica. Who's _____ manager?
e I'm Carla, and this is Natalia. _____ are managers.

**6** Talk to three people. Ask and answer the questions and complete the table below.

*What's your name?*   *Can you spell your surname?*   *What's your manager's name?*

| Person | First name | Surname | Manager |
|---|---|---|---|
| 1 |  |  |  |
| 2 |  |  |  |
| 3 |  |  |  |

# 01 Sara, this is Ed

## Vocabulary

### Introductions

**1** Complete the conversation with *please* or *thank you*.

A: Hello, I'm Francesca Cattagneo.
B: Can you spell your surname, _____?
A: Yes, it's C – A – T – T – A – G – N – E – O.
B: _____.

**2** Match the sentences (a–d) to the replies (1–4).

a  What's your name?          1  Nice to meet you.
b  Sara, this is Ed.          2  You too.
c  Good to meet you, Vicky.   3  Great to meet you, Tom.
d  I'm Tom.                   4  It's Bella Culver.

**3** Complete the conversations using the language in the box.

| Good to meet you | Hello, I'm | It's | This is | What's |

a  Mike:    _____ Mike.
   Sandy:   _____, Mike. I'm Sandy.
   Mike:    Nice to meet you too.

b  Carla:   Hi, Sandra. Great event!
   Sandra:  Yes. Oh, Carla, _____ Cassie.
   Carla:   Hello, Cassie. Good to meet you.
   Cassie:  You too.

c  Mia:     Hello. _____ your name?
   Ella:    _____ Ella.
   Mia:     Nice to meet you.

**4** Write the people's names and companies on the name badge using the correct capital letters.

a  jane radcliffe / british gas
b  adira nadim / saudi aramco
c  chen chi / festival flowers

Name: *Jane* *Radcliffe*
Company: _____

Name: _____
Company: _____

Name: _____
Company: _____

**5** 🔊 1.11 Listen and tick (✓) the names you hear.

Verity Sambell ☐      Jasmine Soutern ☐
Melanie Smith ☐       Michael Steinbeck ☐
Antony Sneed ☐        Gary Swales ☐

## Grammar

### Questions and answers using *be*

**1** Match the sentence beginnings (a–c) to their endings (1–3) to make questions.

a  What's your         1  your manager?
b  Can you             2  surname?
c  Is Tom              3  spell that, please?

**2** Circle the correct word to complete the sentences.

a  That's Sara. *She / She's* my colleague.
b  No, *I / I'm* André.
c  Is Akiko *you're / your* manager? Yes, she is.
d  Hi, *I / I'm* Ed.
e  Are you Charles? Yes, *I'm / I am*.

**3** Circle the correct answer.

a  Are you Adam Lee?          Yes, *I am / it is*.
b  What's your name?          *I'm / This is* Véronique D'Argent.
c  Is she your boss?          Yes, *he is / she is*.
d  Who is your web developer? *This is / It's* Brian Paquot.

**4** Complete the table with the correct long and short forms.

| | Long form | Short form |
|---|---|---|
|   | I am | I'm |
| a |  | you're |
| b | she is/he is | ___ / ___ |
| c |  | it's |
| d |  | we're |
| e | you are |  |
| f | they are |  |

**5** Circle the correct long or short form.

a  Hello, *I'm / I am* Vicky.
b  Are you Mr Porter? Yes, *I'm / I am*.
c  Are you from Expo Solutions? Yes, *we're / we are*.
d  Is he your manager? Yes, *he is / he's*.

**6** Write the correct pronoun.

Hello, (a) _____'m Stella Bryony. Are (b) _____ the head of events? No, (c) _____'m the manager. The head of events is over there. (d) _____'s called Sara. You can go and talk to (e) _____.

## LANGUAGE LINKS

### Pronunciation

**Spelling names**

1  Read and say the alphabet.

A B C D E F G H I J K L M N O P Q R S T U V W X Y Z

2  Cover 1 above and say the alphabet.

3  1.12 Listen and circle the words/phrases you hear.
a  Hi, *I / I'm* David. Good to meet you.
b  My manager is Juan. *He's / His* great.
c  Can you spell your surname, please?
   Certainly. It's *G-A-L-E / J-O-L-E*.
d  Hello, Sarah. Is Jeremy *you / your* manager?
e  *A / Are* you Ahmed?
   No, I'm Mohammed.
f  Kate, *this is / it is* Gunter. Gunter, meet Kate.

4  1.13 Listen and write the names you hear.
a  _____
b  _____
c  _____
d  _____

**Phrase bank: Introducing people**

Circle the correct answer.
a  What's your name?
   *It's Beth. / Good to meet you.*
b  Hello, I'm Stephen.
   *Nice to meet you. / What's your name?*
c  Sara, this is Fatma.
   *It's Juan. / Hello! Great to meet you.*

### Using language

Match each question (a–c) to the reason why you use it (1–3).

a  What's your name?          1  To ask someone to
b  Sara, this is Ed.             spell their name
c  Can you spell your         2  To ask someone's name
   name, please?              3  To introduce people

### Writing

**Completing a name badge**

1  Complete your name badge.

Name: _____  _____
Company: _____

2  Complete the text about yourself.
I'm _____. My surname
is _____. My manager is
_____.

### Reviewing objectives

Tick (✓) the statements which are true for you.

I can say the alphabet in English. ☐
I can introduce myself and other people. ☐
I can ask other people their name. ☐

## My notes from Unit 01

# 02

*The only routine with me is no routine at all.*

Jackie Kennedy Onassis, former First Lady of the United States

**Circle** the word which describes Jackie Kennedy Onassis best. This person is *organized / disorganized*.

**Learning objectives: Unit 2**

**Business communication skills** Using numbers and times; Looking at work routines
Fluency: Talking about your daily work routine
**Reading** Text messages; Article about a typical day in the office
**Listening** Conversations about daily routines
**Vocabulary** Numbers and work-related verbs
**Grammar** Present Simple with key words for work; Questions with *When*, *What time* and *How many*
**Phrase bank** Telling the time
In Company interviews Units 1–2

# I start work at 8 am

## Numbers

1  **1.14** Listen and repeat the numbers.

2  Match each number to a word.

| 1 | four  | 6  | eight   | 11 | fifteen  | 16 | nineteen  |
|---|-------|----|---------|----|----------|----|-----------|
| 2 | three | 7  | ten     | 12 | eleven   | 17 | eighteen  |
| 3 | one   | 8  | six     | 13 | thirteen | 18 | twenty    |
| 4 | five  | 9  | seven   | 14 | fourteen | 19 | sixteen   |
| 5 | two   | 10 | nine    | 15 | twelve   | 20 | seventeen |

3  **1.15** Listen and (circle) the number you hear.

a  12 / 20   c  5 / 15   e  8 / 18
b  3 / 13    d  7 / 17   f  6 / 16

4  Work with a partner and point to a number in 2 for your partner to say.

5  Read the text messages from Dietmar and Pawel. Complete their calendars using the words in the box.

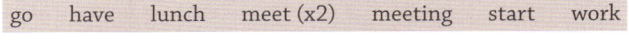
go   have   lunch   meet (x2)   meeting   start   work

Hi Dietmar, can we meet early tomorrow morning? I start work at 8 am. We have a team meeting at 9 am every Monday, so can we meet at 8 am?

Sorry, Pawel, I go to the gym at 8 am. We always have a team meeting at 10 am and I have lunch at 12 pm. Can we meet at 2 pm?

Okay, we can meet at 2 pm but I leave work at 3 pm, okay?

Okay, see you at 2 pm.

Delivered

**10th**  **MONDAY**

| Pawel | |
|---|---|
| 08:00 | _____ work |
| 09:00 | Have a team _____ |
| 14:00 | _____ Dietmar |
| 15:00 | Leave _____ |

**10th**  **MONDAY**

| Dietmar | |
|---|---|
| 08:00 | _____ to gym |
| 10:00 | _____ a team meeting |
| 12:00 | Have _____ |
| 14:00 | _____ Pawel |

6  Write sentences about your day at work using the ideas in 5.

I have _____ at _____.
I start _____ at _____.
I leave _____ at _____.

7  Work with a partner and talk about your day at work using the sentences in 6.

I start work at 8 am.   Really? I start work at 9 am.

I have lunch at 12 pm.   I see. I have lunch at 1 pm.

**BUSINESS COMMUNICATION**

## Telling the time

**1** **1.16** Look at each clock and listen to the time.

**2** **1.16** Match the clocks (a–f) to the times (1–6). Listen again and check.

1  quarter past two
2  quarter to seven
3  half past four
4  ten past three
5  five to ten
6  three o'clock

**3** **1.17** Listen to Colin and Julia talking about their daily routine. Complete the table using the times in the box.

1.15   12.50   8.30   9.00

|  | Colin | Julia |
|---|---|---|
| Start work |  |  |
| Have lunch |  |  |

### Writing tips

Start each sentence with a capital letter.

*Can we meet early tomorrow morning?*

Correct these sentences using capital letters.

a  i can meet at 5 pm today.
b  i have a meeting at 5 pm. can we meet in the morning?

**4** **1.17** Listen again and complete the conversation.

**Colin:** (a) _____ do you start work?
**Julia:** At nine o'clock. What about you, (b) _____ time do you start work?
**Colin:** At half past eight.
**Julia:** What (c) _____ do you have lunch?
**Colin:** Um, at ten to one. And you, (d) _____ do you have lunch?
**Julia:** Quarter past one.

> **QUESTION TIME**
> Complete the questions below with the missing words.
> When _____ check your emails?
> What time _____ leave work?

**5** Write questions with *you*, using the information below.

a  When / start work

b  What time / check your emails

c  What time / have a team meeting

d  When / have lunch

e  When / leave work

**6** Ask your classmates about their day at work using the questions in 5.

> When do you start work?

> At nine o'clock.

**02 I START WORK AT 8 AM**   15

## Talk, Talk, Talk ...

JANNIE HELIN, MANAGER

a

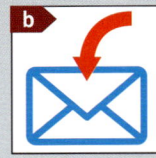
b

c

d

e

## A day in the life ...

**1** Read the magazine article and circle the correct answer for each statement.

a Business people *talk a lot / don't talk a lot*.
b Spoken communication *is important / isn't important* in business.
c Jannie Helin *has / doesn't have* a lot of meetings.

Talking is very important for business people. Research shows they spend 18 minutes an hour at work talking. Jannie Helin is a busy woman. Most days, she doesn't have time for lunch! She receives about 20 emails an hour but only replies to 10. She also makes and receives around 15 phone calls a day. She has between 6 and 12 meetings a week. With all this time talking, how do business people have time to work?

**2** Match the numbers from the text to the pictures (a–e).

20 ☐    18 ☐    10 ☐    15 ☐    6–12 ☐

**3** Read the sentences below and circle the correct verb.

| Positive | Negative | have |
|---|---|---|
| I *check / checks* my emails in the morning. | I *don't / doesn't* check my emails in the morning. | I *have / has* a meeting every morning. |
| You *check / checks* your emails in the morning. | You *don't / doesn't* check your emails in the morning. | You *have / has* a meeting every morning. |
| She *check / checks* her emails in the morning. | He *don't / doesn't* check his emails in the morning. | She *have / has* a meeting every morning. |
| They *check / checks* their emails in the morning. | They *don't / doesn't* check their emails in the morning. | They *have / has* a meeting every morning. |

**4** Complete the sentences using the verb in brackets.

a I _____ 20 emails a day. (send)
b John _____ three meetings today. (have)
c They _____ any phone calls. (not make)
d She _____ 15 phone calls a day. (not receive)

**5** 🔊 **1.18** Listen and check your answers.

**6** Use the information below to write three sentences about your job.

| Verbs | Nouns | Time periods |
|---|---|---|
| have; make; receive; reply to; send | emails; meetings; phone calls | a day; an hour; a week |

_____
_____
_____

**7** Work with a partner and talk about your work routine using the sentences in 6.

> I send five emails a day.

> I send ten emails a day.

> I make four phone calls an hour.

> I make one phone call an hour.

BUSINESS COMMUNICATION

## A coffee break conversation

**1**  1.19 Colin and Julia are on a coffee break. Listen to the conversation and tick (✓) the things they talk about.

emails ☐   meetings ☐   phone calls ☐   starting work ☐

> 💬 **Natural language**
> When we answer questions about routines, we often use *about* or *around* + a number:
> 💬 How many emails do you send a day?
> 💬 About/Around 20.

**2** 1.19 Listen again and complete the conversation.

**Colin:** Hi, how are you?
**Julia:** Fine – busy, though. I have a lot of emails to read.
**Colin:** Really? How (a) _____ emails do you receive?
**Julia:** Um, about (b) _____ a day. What about you, how many emails (c) _____ you receive?
**Colin:** Around ten. What about phone calls, (d) _____ many phone calls do you make?
**Julia:** About (e) _____ a day. What about you?
**Colin:** Um, about eight. And how many phone calls (f) _____ you receive?
**Julia:** Around (g) _____, but they're long. I spend a lot of time on the phone.

### ❓ QUESTION TIME
**Complete the questions.**
How _____ emails _____ receive?
_____ meetings _____ have?
_____ phone calls _____ make?

**3** Match the sentence beginnings (a–d) to the endings (1–4).

a  How many emails            1  do you have a week?
b  How many phone calls       2  do you receive a day?
c  How many meetings          3  do you make a day?
d  How many emails            4  do you send a day?

**4** Work with a partner. Using the sentences in 3, ask and answer questions to complete the table below.

| You | | Your partner | |
|---|---|---|---|
| send / email / day | *I send 15 emails a day.* | send / email / day | *He sends ten emails a day.* |
| receive / email / day | | receive / email / day | |
| make / phone call / day | | make / phone call / day | |
| have meeting / week | | have meeting / week | |

In Company interviews Units 1–2

**5** Work with a new partner and tell them about your partner in 4.

> Rodrigo sends ten emails a day.

**02 I START WORK AT 8 AM**  17

# 02 I start work at 8 am

**Vocabulary**

## Numbers and work-related verbs

**1** 🔊 **1.20** Listen and write the numbers you hear. There are two numbers in each sentence.

a _13_ / _20_
b ____ / ____
c ____ / ____
d ____ / ____
e ____ / ____
f ____ / ____

**2** 🔊 **1.21** Now listen to the numbers and repeat.

**3** Match the verbs in the box to a noun below.

| check | finish | have | ~~make~~ | receive (x2) |
| reply to | send | start | | |

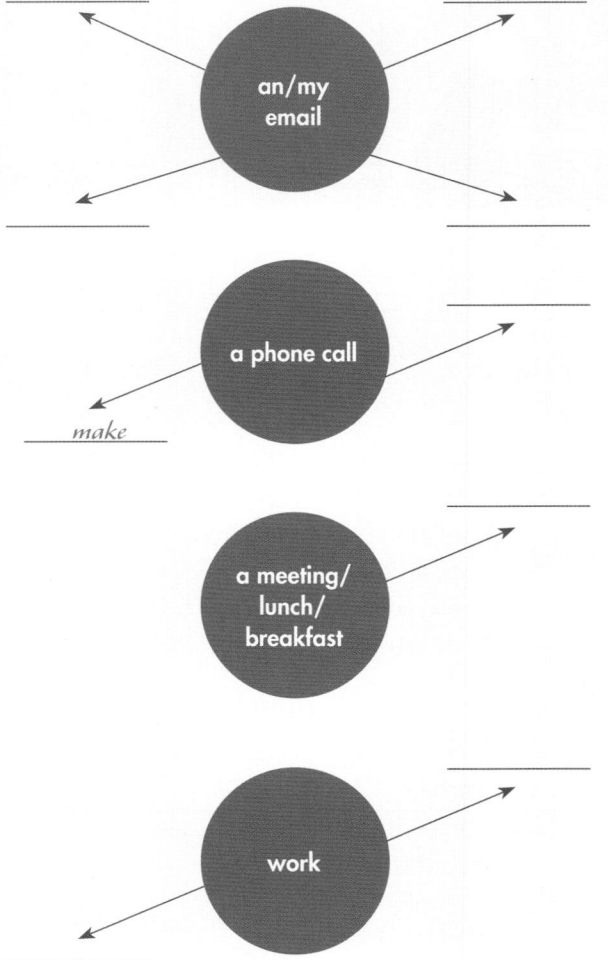

**Grammar**

## Present Simple

**1** Read the information in the table.

| Positive | Negative | *have* |
| --- | --- | --- |
| I make phone calls. | I don't make phone calls. | I have a meeting. |
| You make phone calls. | You don't make phone calls. | You have a meeting. |
| He/She makes phone calls. | He/She doesn't make phone calls. | He/She has a meeting. |
| We make phone calls. | We don't make phone calls. | We have a meeting. |
| They make phone calls. | They don't make phone calls. | They have a meeting. |

**2** Write sentences using the information below and the correct verb form.

a John / send / 20 emails a day
_____

b I / have / three meetings today
_____

c You / make / nine phone calls a day
_____

d We / have / six meetings a week
_____

e I / not send / any emails
_____

f He / make / six phone calls a day
_____

**3** Complete the questions with the words in the box.

| do (x2) | many (x2) | time | when |

a _____ do you check your emails?
b How _____ meetings do you have a week?
c What time _____ you start work?
d How many phone calls _____ you make a day?
e What _____ do you finish work?
f How _____ emails do you receive a day?

## LANGUAGE LINKS

### Pronunciation

#### Questions

1 **1.22** Listen and underline the *unstressed* words.
a When <u>do you</u> start work?
b What time do you have lunch?
c How many phone calls do you receive a day?
d When do you finish work?
e When do you wake up?

2 **1.22** Listen again and repeat the sentences.

### Using language

Match each question beginning (a–c) to the reason why you use it (1–2).

a When …    1 To ask questions about quantity
b How many …    2 To ask questions about time
c What time …

### Phrase bank: Telling the time

1 **1.23** Listen and tick (✓) the times you hear.

half past four ☐    quarter to seven ☐
ten past eight ☐    quarter past one ☐
ten past five ☐    half past six ☐

2 **1.23** Listen again and repeat the sentences.
3 Write the matching time from 1 under each clock below.

A

B

_____    _____

C

_____

### Writing

#### Your calendar

Use the information from Jannie's calendar to write sentences about her day, then do the same for yourself.

| 09:00 | start work |
| 10:00 | have a team meeting |
| 11:00 | make phone calls |
| 12:00 | have lunch |
| 13:00 | check emails |
| 17:00 | leave work |

| 1 | Jannie | 2 | Me |
|---|---|---|---|
| 09:00 | *Jannie starts work at 9 am.* | : | *I start work at _____ am.* |
| 10:00 | | : | |
| 11:00 | | : | |
| 12:00 | | : | |
| 13:00 | | : | |
| 17:00 | | : | |

### Reviewing objectives

Tick (✓) the statements which are true for you.

I can count to 20. ☐
I can tell the time. ☐
I can talk about my day at work. ☐
I can ask questions about daily routines. ☐

## My notes from Unit 02

# SURVIVAL SCENARIO A

## Learning objectives: Survival Scenario A

**Business communication skills**
Checking in to a hotel; Asking questions about hotel facility opening times and locations; Roleplay: Checking in to a hotel and asking about the facilities
**Reading** Email about travel plans
**In Company in action**
A1: Welcome to The Western Hotel;
A2: I have a few questions

# Enjoy your stay!

a _____  b _____  c _____

e _____

f _____

**1** Label the photos using the words in the box.

| breakfast | café | guest | gym | lift |
| passport | receptionist | restaurant | | |

d _____

g _____

h _____

**2** Antonio is the overseas sales manager for BetterDrinks and it is his first visit to the UK. Work with a partner. Read the email and take turns to ask and answer the questions.

---

**To:** Antonio Dias
**From:** Karl Harrison
**Date:** 8 May

Dear Antonio,

Thank you for your email. I hope you are well. I am very excited about our new product – Bubble tea. It's from Taiwan. We can talk about it at our meeting on Tuesday. I've now got the details about your visit to London. Julie tells me it's your first visit here! Your hotel is The Western Hotel in Lulworth Street in central London. You arrive at London Heathrow Airport on Monday 16th May at 11.30 am. A taxi will meet you at the airport, and can take you to the hotel. I hope this is okay.

Karl

Karl Harrison
Sales Manager
BetterDrinks UK

---

a  Who is the email from?
b  Who is the email to?
c  What is the name of Antonio's hotel?
d  Where is Antonio's hotel?
e  When does he arrive at the airport?

# SURVIVAL SCENARIO

In Company in action

**3** Antonio checks in to his hotel in London. Watch video A1 and circle the correct answer.
a Antonio's room is on the *second / third* floor.
b Antonio wants to eat *lunch / dinner*.

**4** Watch video A1 again and complete the receptionist's form.

> **W H** The Western Hotel LONDON
>
> Name: (a) _____ (first name)
>      (b) _____ (surname)
> Nights:   1   2   3   4
> Passport number: (c) _____

**5** Match the sentences (a–e) to the numbers (1–5).
a Your room number is three oh two.     **1** 3rd
b That's on the third floor.            **2** 19:00
c It's open until 3 pm.                 **3** 2nd
d It opens at seven o'clock this evening. **4** 15:00
e It's on the second floor.             **5** 302

**6** In a hotel, who says these phrases? Write *R* (receptionist) or *G* (guest).
a How can I help you?                                    *R*
b I have a few questions.                                ___
c What can I help you with?                              ___
d Where is the swimming pool?                            ___
e When is breakfast?                                     ___
f Is the gym open now?                                   ___
g The restaurant opens at 7 pm and closes at 11.30.      ___
h Enjoy your stay.                                       ___

In Company in action

**7** Antonio is back at the reception desk. Watch video A2 and tick (✓) the phrases from 6 that you hear.

**8** Fill in the missing information. Watch Video A2 again to check your answers.

The Café – Ground floor: Opens at 11 am and closes at 3 pm
The Restaurant – (a) _5th_ floor
Breakfast from (b) _____ am to (c) _____ am
Dinner from (d) _____ pm to (e) _____ pm
The Gym (f) – _____ floor: Opens at 8 am and closes at (g) _____ pm

**9** Work with a partner and practise the conversations on page 87. Take turns being the receptionist and the guest.

**10** Two guests check in to The Western Hotel. Work with a partner and roleplay the conversations.
Speaker A: Look at page 88.        Speaker B: Look at page 83.

Evaluate your performance using the Reviewing objectives box on page 85.

**A ENJOY YOUR STAY!**

# 03

> There is only one boss. The customer.
>
> Sam Walton, founder of Walmart

**According to Sam Walton, how important is the customer?** Circle the correct answer.
*Very important / quite important / not very important*

**Learning objectives: Unit 3**
**Business communication skills** Looking at jobs and companies
Fluency: Talking about your job and your company
**Reading** Work the Net profiles
**Listening** Conversations about jobs, sectors and companies
**Vocabulary** Jobs, sectors and numbers *10–100* (tens), *100–1,000* (hundreds), *10,000–50,000* (thousands)
**Grammar** Questions with *do/does*
**Phrase bank** Describing your job and company

# Where do you work?

## Talking about work

**1** 1.24 Listen to a conversation at a conference and circle the correct answer.
a Daniel Almeida is from *Paris / São Paulo / St Lucia*.
b Daniel works for *Appetizer / Apple / Acer*.
c He's a *computer programmer / receptionist / technician*.

**2** 1.24 Listen again and complete the sentences using *do* or *are*.
a Where _____ you from?        1 _____
b Where _____ you work?        2 _____
c What _____ you do?           3 _____

**3** Write these answers to the questions on the correct lines in 2 above.
*I'm a technician.    I'm from São Paulo.    I work for Appetizer.*

**4** Read the listening script on page 90 and check your answers.

**5** Talk to five other students. Ask and answer the questions below.

> Where are you from?    Where do you work?

## Jobs

**1** Match the jobs in the box to the photos and circle *a* or *an*.

engineer    hotel manager    human resources manager
receptionist    sales manager    taxi driver

a  She's *a /an* _____

b  He's *a /an* _____

c  She's *a /an* _____

d  She's *a /an* _____

e  He's *a /an* _____

f  She's *a /an* _____

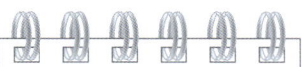

**Writing tips**

Use a full stop at the end of sentences.

*I'm from Hong Kong.*
*I work for HSBC.*

Use a question mark at the end of questions.

*Where do you work?*
*What do you do?*

Write the correct punctuation (full stop or question mark) in these sentences.

a  I'm a technician
b  What's your name
c  Can you speak Spanish
d  She's from Brazil

**2** 1.25 Listen to the two conversations and write the people's jobs.

**Michael:** He's a _____.
**Sara:** She's a _____.

**3** 1.25 Listen again and complete the sentences.

Michael *works* for Emirates Airlines.

a  Michael _____ the phone.
b  Sara _____ company training sessions.

**4** Work in groups. Ask and answer the questions below.

Where are you from?   I'm from Moscow.   What do you do?   I'm a technician.

## Work profiles

**1** Read the Work the Net profiles and answer the questions.

a  Where is Misha Watanabe from?  _____
b  What does Antony Bradley do?  _____
c  Where does Misha Watanabe work?  _____

**Misha Watanabe**
Human Resources Manager
Tokyo, Japan
**Current** Sony

**Antony Bradley**
Website Designer
London, UK
**Current** PrimeSite

**2** Choose one profile. Write sentences about him/her.

*Antony is from London. He's a ...*

_____
_____

**3** Work with a new partner and take turns to ask and answer the questions below. Take notes.

Where are you from?   Where do you work?   What do you do?

**4** Complete the description about your partner.

_____ (name and surname) is from _____ (city/country).
_____ (first name) works for _____ (company).
He's/She's a _____ (job).

**5** Tell the class about your partner.

## Sectors

**1** Match the sectors to the photos (a–f).

construction ☐   energy ☐   finance ☐   retail ☐   telecoms ☐   tourism ☐

**2** Complete the sentences with your job, the sector you work in and your company.
I'm a/an _____.   I work in _____.   I work for _____.

**3** 🔊 1.26 Listen and tick (✓) the sectors you hear.
energy ☐   finance ☐   retail ☐   telecoms ☐

**4** 🔊 1.26 Listen again and circle the correct sector for each person.
a  Carlo is in *energy / finance / retail / telecoms*.
b  Estella is in *energy / finance / retail / telecoms*.

**5** 🔊 1.26 Listen again and circle the *two* correct answers for each question.
a  Where does Estella work? *She works for Corieza. / She trains staff. / In Buenos Aires.*
b  What does Estella do? *She's a human resources manager. / In Buenos Aires. / She trains staff.*

> **QUESTION TIME**
> Complete the questions using the words in the box.
>
> are   do (x3)   is
>
> a  Where _____ you from?
> b  Where _____ you work?
> c  What _____ you _____?
> d  How big _____ your company?

## Questions about people at work

**1** Complete the questions with *do* or *does*.
a  Where _____ he work?
b  What _____ you do?
c  What does she _____?
d  Where _____ Sara work?

**2** Complete the sentences with *am/'m*, *is/'s* or *are/'re*.
a  Where _____ she from?
b  I _____ from Paris.
c  He _____ from the Emirates.
d  They _____ from France.

**3** Complete the table using the correct verb forms.

|  | The verb *be* (full) | The verb *be* (short) | The verb *do* |
|---|---|---|---|
| I | am |  | do |
| you |  | 're |  |
| he/she | is |  |  |
| we |  | 're | do |
| you |  |  | do |
| they | are |  |  |

💬 **Natural language**
When talking about our work, we often use the expressions *I work in ...* or *I'm in ...* plus the sector (*banking, tourism*):
- 💬 *I'm in food production.*
- 💬 *Oh, really? I'm in human resources.*
- 💬 *I work in the retail sector.*
- 💬 *I see. I work in finance.*

03 WHERE DO YOU WORK?

BUSINESS COMMUNICATION

**4** Match the sentence beginnings (a–d) to the endings (1–4).

a  What does          1  she work?
b  How big            2  she do?
c  Where does         3  she from?
d  Where's            4  is Corieza?

**5** Work with a partner. Ask and answer questions about Estella.

> Where does she work?

> She works for Corieza.

## Tens, hundreds, thousands

**1** 1.27 Read and listen to the numbers.

a  10    20    30    40    50    60    70    80    90    100
b  100   200   300   400   500   600   700   800   900   1,000
c  100   1,000   10,000
d  500   5,000   50,000

**2** Work with a partner. Take turns to say a number from 1 and have your partner point to it.

**3** 1.28 Listen and circle the numbers you hear.

a  3 / 30          e  400 / 4,000         i  40,000 / 50,000
b  50 / 500        f  100 / 1,000         j  1,000 / 10,000
c  30 / 40         g  60 / 60,000
d  300 / 500       h  8 / 80

## How big is your company?

**1** How big is your company? Circle the word which best describes your company.

My company is *small / medium-sized / big*.

**2** 1.29 Listen and complete the information for Freddie.

|                | Freddie     | Abdullah         |
|----------------|-------------|------------------|
| Job            |             | *flight attendant* |
| Company        | *Dream Build* |                  |
| Sector         |             |                  |
| Size of company |            |                  |

**3** 1.29 Listen again and check your answers.

**4** 1.30 Listen and tick (✓) the questions you hear.

a  What do you do? ☐             c  Who is your boss? ☐
b  Where do you work? ☐          d  How big is it? ☐

**5** 1.30 Listen again and complete the information for Abdullah.

**6** Work with a partner. Ask questions about their job and company.

> Where do you work?

> How big is your company?

**7** Work with a new partner. Tell them about your first partner's work and company.

> Aylin is in finance. She works for Lloyds Bank. She's a …

03 WHERE DO YOU WORK?

# 03 Where do you work?

## Vocabulary

### Jobs, sectors and numbers

**1** Complete the sentences with the words in the box and (circle) *a* or *an*.

| engineer | hotel manager | human resources manager |
| receptionist | sales manager | taxi driver |

a   Nadia is *a / an* _____. She plans sales and works with marketing staff.
b   Marco is *a / an* _____. He fixes computer systems.
c   Lena works as *a / an* _____. She answers the phone.
d   Javier is *a / an* _____. He drives people around the city.
e   Carmen is *a / an* _____. She works with all the staff in the hotel.
f   Liv is *a / an* _____. She trains new staff.

**2**  1.31 Listen and match the people to the sectors in the box.

| construction | energy | finance | tourism |

a   Maya     _____
b   Selma    _____
c   Marion   _____
d   Georgio  _____

**3** Match the words (a–f) to the numbers (1–6).

a   four thousand      1   15
b   fourteen           2   70
c   seventy            3   300
d   forty              4   4,000
e   fifteen            5   14
f   three hundred      6   40

## Grammar

### Questions and answers about your job and company

**1** Put the words in the correct order to make questions with *do* and *be*. Remember to add question marks.

a   do you what do
_____
b   from where you are
_____
c   company is big how your
_____
d   do where work you
_____

**2** Match the sentence beginnings (a–c) to the endings (1–3).

a   Where do you work?      1   I work for Siemens.
b   Where are you from?     2   I'm an engineer.
c   What do you do?         3   I'm from Frankfurt.

**3** Complete the sentences with *work* or *works*.

a   I _____ for Vodafone.
b   Where do you _____ ?
c   Saskia _____ in Istanbul.
d   He _____ for Apple.

**4** Write the questions (a–d) for the answers.

a   *Where do you work?*
    I work in Riyadh.
b   _____
    It has 25 employees.
c   _____
    I train new staff.
d   _____
    I'm from Saudi Arabia.

## Pronunciation

### Numbers

**1** Say the following numbers.

| 13 | 30 | 300 | 3,000 |
| 7  | 70 | 17  | 1,700 |
| 16 | 60 | 6   | 6,000 |

**2**  1.32 Listen and check.

**3**  1.33 Listen and write the numbers you hear.

a   _____
b   _____
c   _____
d   _____
e   _____

# LANGUAGE LINKS

**Phrase bank: Talking about your job and your company**

Circle the correct answer.

a  Where are you from?
   *I'm in telecoms. / I'm from Brazil.*
b  Where do you work?
   *I work for Total Telecoms. / I'm a technician.*
c  What do you do?
   *I'm from Turkey. / I'm a sales manager.*
d  How big is your company?
   *It has about 2,000 employees. / I work in finance.*

## Using language

Tick (✓) the correct column in the table.

|  | Asking about a person's work | Asking for personal information |
|---|---|---|
| What's your name? |  | ✓ |
| Where do you work? | ✓ |  |
| Where are you from? |  |  |
| What do you do? |  |  |
| How big is your company? |  |  |

## Writing

**About you and your company**

**1** Complete the text about yourself.

My name is (a) _____. I'm in (b) _____. I work for (c) _____. It has about (d) _____ employees. I'm a(n) (e) _____.

**2** Match the gaps above (a–e) to the information below (1–5).

1  company size    ___
2  sector          ___
3  job             ___
4  name            ___
5  company         ___

## Reviewing objectives

Tick (✓) the statements which are true for you.

I can talk about my job and my company. ☐

I can understand and ask simple questions with *Where*, *What* and *How*. ☐

I can understand and use numbers (10s, 100s and 1,000s). ☐

# My notes from Unit 03

# 04

> *I don't answer the phone. I get the feeling when I do someone will want to speak to me.*
>
> Fred Couples, golfer

Circle the correct answer.
Fred Couples *doesn't like / likes* talking on the phone.

**Learning objectives: Unit 4**
**Business communication skills** Making simple telephone calls; Making arrangements; Roleplay: Leaving a message; Fluency: Talking about dates
**Listening** Telephone calls to leave a message and to arrange a meeting
**Vocabulary** Telephone numbers; Dates, days and months
**Grammar** *Can* for requests and possibility
**Phrase bank** Telephone phrases
**In Company interviews** Units 3–4

# Can I help you?

## Telephone calls

1  1.34 Listen to Kristina Müller making a phone call and tick (✓) the correct phone number.

01623 303 5448 ☐    01643 202 6449 ☐    01743 404 5610 ☐

**QUESTION TIME**
Complete the telephone questions below with the missing word.

_____ I help you?
I ask who's calling?
I take a message?
he call Kristina Müller?

1.34 Listen again and check your answers.

2  Match the sentence beginnings (a–g) to the endings (1–7) to make common telephone phrases.

a  Can I speak to        1  who's calling?
b  How can I             2  anything else?
c  Mr Smith is           3  Kristina Müller, please?
d  Can I ask             4  a message?
e  Can I take            5  Mr Smith, please?
f  Is there              6  help you?
g  Can he call           7  out of the office today.

3  Look at the questions in 2 and decide if the statement below is true (T) or false (F).
We ask questions with *can* to see if something is possible.    T / F

28    04 CAN I HELP YOU?

**BUSINESS COMMUNICATION**

4  **1.35** Listen and label the telephone numbers (a–d) in the order you hear them.

+12 997 541 3324  ____    +41 608 587 4477  ____
0044 208 648 7559  ____    0088 887 707 6841  ____

## Leaving a message

1  Rearrange the words in each box to make a telephone conversation.

A                                                                                                                B

1  morning good / help I can how you?
   *Good morning. How can I help you?*

   2  I speak can to please **Paul Smith**? _____

3  he's sorry **of the out office**. _____

4  I can you help? _____

   5  thanks no / will be he when back? _____

6  **tomorrow** / a message take can I? _____

   7  please yes / call can he me on **0044 788 480 5945** _____

8  okay that's so **0044 788 480 5945** _____

   9  that's yes right _____

10  is anything there else? _____

   11  **no bye thanks** _____

12  bye okay _____

> **Natural language**
>
> When two numbers together are the same in a telephone number, we often say *double*.
> 33 = *double three*
> 88 = _____ *eight*
> It is also very common in telephone numbers to say *oh* instead of *zero*.
> 0207 = *oh two oh seven*
> 001 = *double oh one*
> Practise saying these telephone numbers with your partner.
> 0081 445 087 5441
> 0029 352 698 7411

2  Work with a partner and practise the telephone call.

3  Replace the **bold** text in 1 using the information below to make new conversations. With your partner take turns being A and B.

A                                                                                                                B

3  in a meeting / out at lunch                                    2  Daniel Gelder / Tom Price

6  this afternoon / next week                                    7  020 5324 1643 / 01789 417 863

8  020 5324 1643 / 01789 417 863                           11  That's all, thanks. / No, that's great.

04  CAN I HELP YOU?   29

Time:
Day:

## Are you free on Tuesday?

**1** 1.36 Listen to the telephone conversation and write the time and day of the meeting on the notepad.

**2** 1.36 Complete these extracts from the phone call in 1 with *can/can't*. Listen again and check your answers.

a Hello, _____ I speak to Kristina, please?
b Oh, I _____ meet in the afternoon.
c I _____ do 3.00 pm.

**3** Match each example in 2 to a meaning below.
1 It isn't possible.   *b*
2 Is it possible?   ___
3 It is possible.   ___

**4** Use *can/can't* to complete the sentences and match the meaning of the symbol.
✓ it is possible   ? is it possible   ✗ it isn't possible

a ? *Can* I speak to Chris please?
b ✓ I _____ go to the meeting.
c ✗ I _____ go to the meeting.
d ✗ I _____ meet at 3 pm.
e ? _____ you meet at 3 pm?
f ✓ I _____ meet at 4 pm.

**5** Complete the table with *can / can't*

| Postive | Negative | Question |
|---|---|---|
| I | I | I …? |
| You | You | you …? |
| He/She/It _____ | He/She/It _____ | _____ he/she/it …? |
| We | We | we …? |
| They | They | they …? |

## Days, months and dates

**1** Put the days of the week in the correct order.

Tuesday ___   Thursday ___   Sunday ___   Monday *1*
Wednesday ___   Friday ___   Saturday ___

**2** 1.37 Listen and check your answers.

**3** 1.37 Listen again and repeat the days of the week.

**4** Label each photo with words in the box.

afternoon   evening   morning   night

8:00am    2:00pm    6:00pm    9:00pm

**BUSINESS COMMUNICATION**

**5** Work with a partner. Choose a day of the week and time of day and take turns to guess their choice.

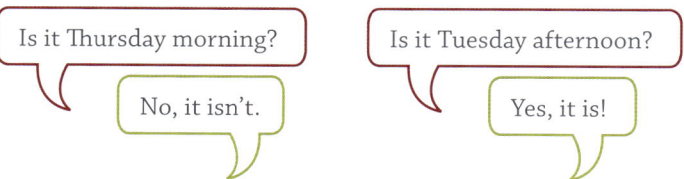

**6** Put the months in the correct order.

| | | | | | | | |
|---|---|---|---|---|---|---|---|
| January | 1 | August | ___ | September | ___ | April | ___ |
| October | ___ | March | ___ | May | ___ | December | ___ |
| July | ___ | June | ___ | November | ___ | February | ___ |

**7** 1.38 Listen and check your answers.

**8** 1.39 Listen to people talking about important events. Match the dates to a speaker.

a 1st January        Speaker 1: _c_
b 22nd February   Speaker 2: ___
c 3rd April              Speaker 3: ___
d 6th November   Speaker 4: ___
e 18th August        Speaker 5: ___

**Writing tips**

When we say the date, we normally use *the* and *of*:
*the tenth of May*
When we write the date, we use the number and month only:
*10th May*
We can include the year:
*10th May 2015*
We can also leave out the *th* (or *st/nd/rd*):
*10 May 2015*

**9** Write the date of these events in your life.

Your birthday                                                     _____
An important public holiday in your country   _____
The birthday of someone in your family          _____

**10** Work with a partner and tell them the dates in 9.

My birthday's on the 24th of November.

**11** 1.40 Listen to Kristina Müller and José González discussing a meeting on the telephone. Tick (✓) the dates you hear.

a 8th August ☐
b 14th July ☐
c 23rd July ☐
d 14th August ☐
e 18th August ☐

**12** 1.40 Listen again and decide if the statements are true (T) or false (F).

a Kristina wants to change the time for the meeting.        T / F
b José is busy on the 18th August.                                         T / F
c Kristina is busy on the 14th August.                                   T / F
d The new date for the meeting is the 18th August.          T / F

**13** Work with a partner and arrange a meeting.

Speaker A: Look at page 82.                Speaker B: Look at page 86.

# 04 Can I help you?

**Vocabulary**

## Telephone numbers, days and months

**1** 🔊 **1.41** Listen and (circle) the four telephone numbers you hear.

0044 208 456 7744   0022 234 3344   0087 285 7459
0028 334 4454       0048 255 8974   0055 778 8992

**2** Write the missing letters to complete the days of the week.

M __ __ day    T __ e __ day    __ edn __ sday
T __ ur __ day    __ r __ day    S __ t __ rday    __ u __ day

**3** Use the ideas in the box to write your weekly routine.

| check my emails | cook dinner | go shopping |
| go to a restaurant | go to the gym | have dinner with my family |
| have meetings | leave work early | meet friends |
| meet my boss | pay my bills | start work early |

Monday      _I start work early on Monday morning._
Tuesday     _____
Wednesday   _____
Thursday    _____
Friday      _____
Saturday    _____
Sunday      _____
Every day   _____

**4** Complete the crossword with the months of the year.

**Across**

1 The 3rd month of the year (M...)
3 The 7th month of the year (J...)
4 The 8th month of the year (Au...)
6 The 11th month of the year (No...)
7 The 4th month of the year (Ap...)
8 The 10th month of the year (Oc...)
9 The 12th month of the year (De...)
10 The 2nd month of the year (Fe...)

**Down**

1 The 5th month of the year (M...)
2 The 1st month of the year (Jan...)
3 The 6th month of the year (Ju...)
5 The 9th month of the year (Se...)

**5** Write the dates in words.

a 22.02   _22nd February_
b 02.08   _____
c 13.12   _____
d 03.03   _____
e 31.01   _____
f 24.05   _____

**6** Write the date of these events in your life.

a Your best friend's birthday   _____
b The day you started school    _____
c The day of a public holiday in your country
  _____

**Grammar**

## Can for requests and possibility

**1** Complete the sentences with *can/can't*.

a _____ we meet on Monday?
b Sorry, I _____. I'm busy.
c I _____ meet on Tuesday. Is that okay?
d I _____ meet in the morning. I have another meeting.
e _____ we meet in the afternoon?
f I'm free then. We _____ meet on Tuesday afternoon.

**2** 🔊 **1.42** Listen and check your answers.

**3** Rewrite the sentences using *can/can't*. Use the icons to help you.

a I am free to meet you on Monday. ✓
  _I can meet you on Monday._
b I am not free to meet you on Monday. ✗
  _____
c Are you free to meet me on Monday? ?
  _____
d It's okay for you to leave early tomorrow. ✓
  _____
e It's not okay for you to leave early tomorrow. ✗
  _____
f Is it okay for me to leave early tomorrow? ?
  _____

## LANGUAGE LINKS

### Using language

Match each example of *can* (a–c) to a meaning (1–3).

| a | I can meet you on Monday. | 1 | It's not possible. |
|---|---|---|---|
| b | Can we meet on Monday? | 2 | It is possible. |
| c | I can't meet on Monday. | 3 | Is it possible? |

### Pronunciation

#### Days and months

**1** Underline the stressed syllable in the days of the week.

| Monday | Thursday | Sunday |
|---|---|---|
| Tuesday | Friday | |
| Wednesday | Saturday | |

**2** 1.43 Listen and check your answers.

**3** Underline the stressed syllable in the months in the year.

| January | April | July | October |
|---|---|---|---|
| February | May | August | November |
| March | June | September | December |

**4** 1.44 Listen and check your answers

#### Phrase bank: Telephone phrases

Complete the conversation with the words in the box.

ask   call   can   else   it's   out   speak   take

A: Good morning, how (a) _____ I help you?
B: Hello, can I (b) _____ to Mr Smith, please?
A: Can I (c) _____ who's calling?
B: (d) _____ Samantha Lyons.
A: I'll just check.
A: I'm sorry, Mr Smith is (e) _____ of the office today. Can I (f) _____ a message?
B: Can he (g) _____ Samantha Lyons, please?
A: No problem. Is there anything (h) _____?
B: No thanks, bye.
A: Bye.

1.45 Listen and check your answers.

### Writing

#### Messages

Complete the message using the information on the call sheet.

| Message for: | Bill |
|---|---|
| Caller: | Samantha Lyons |
| Telephone Number: | 0207 844 558 |
| Time of call: | Fri 3 pm |
| Message: | call back Mon/Tues AM? |

Hi Bill,
Samantha (a) _____ called you.
She called on Friday (b) _____.
She wants you to call (c) _____ back.
Her (d) _____ is 0207 844 558.
(e) _____ you call her
(f) _____ or Tuesday
(g) _____ ?

### Reviewing objectives

Tick (✓) the statements which are true for you.

I can make a telephone call. ☐
I can receive a telephone call. ☐
I can talk about significant dates. ☐
I know the days of the week. ☐
I know the months of the year. ☐

## My notes from Unit 04

# SURVIVAL SCENARIO B

**Learning objectives: Workplace Scenario B**
**Business communication skills** Saying where places are in a town; Saying where places are in an office; Roleplay: Asking where places are in a town
**Reading** Text message about plans to meet
**In Company in action**
B1: I want to get to the office;
B2: Go straight to the meeting room

In Company in action

# It's very close

**1** Look at the map and complete the sentences below.

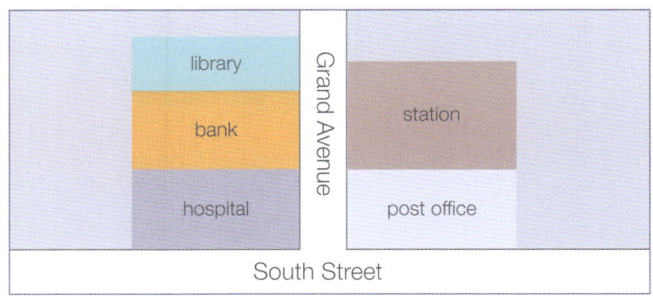

a The station is on *Grand Avenue*.
b The station is next to the _____.
c The station is opposite the _____.
d The bank is between the _____ and the _____.

**2** It is the day of the meeting at BetterDrinks. Karl sends Antonio a text message. Read the message and (circle) the correct answer.

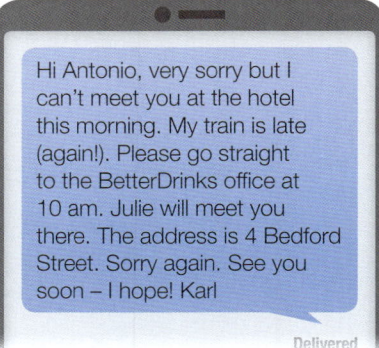

Hi Antonio, very sorry but I can't meet you at the hotel this morning. My train is late (again!). Please go straight to the BetterDrinks office at 10 am. Julie will meet you there. The address is 4 Bedford Street. Sorry again. See you soon – I hope! Karl

a Karl is *in a meeting / at a train station* right now.
b Karl wants Antonio to go to the BetterDrinks office *in ten minutes / at ten o'clock*.
c Julie will meet Antonio at the *office / hotel*.

**3** Antonio is having breakfast when he receives Karl's message. Watch video B1 and decide if the statements are true (T) or false (F).

a The BetterDrinks office is near the hotel.  T / F
b There is a café on Bedford Street.  T / F
c The office is opposite a department store.  T / F

**4** Complete the map with the places in the box. Watch video B1 again to check your answers.

BetterDrinks office    café    ~~department store~~    The Western Hotel

```
                petrol station          (a) _____
                convenience
                  store                  (b) _____
                  bank                   (c) department store
                        Lulworth Street
police station    (d) _____    Italian restaurant    library
```

34  B IT'S VERY CLOSE

## SURVIVAL SCENARIO

**5** Match the phrases (a–d) to the words with the same meaning (1–4).

| a | opposite | 1 | close to |
|---|---|---|---|
| b | near | 2 | in the middle of |
| c | between | 3 | on the right/left of |
| d | next to | 4 | across from |

**6** Here is a short conversation based on the map in 4.

a With a partner, put these sentences in the correct order and practise reading the conversation.
  i   Thanks for your help. ☐
  ii  You're welcome. ☐
  iii It's on <u>Lulworth Street</u>. It's <u>between the Italian restaurant and the police station</u>. ☐
  iv  Excuse me, where is <u>The Western Hotel</u>? ☐ 1

b Change the <u>underlined</u> words to make new conversations. Use the places on the map in 4 and the words in 5 to help you.

**7** Look at the plan of the BetterDrinks office and complete the sentences. Use the words and phrases from 5 to help you.

[Plan: lift (top), kitchen, Karl's office, room A on left side; Caroline's office, room B, Julie's office, room C on right side; Corridor in middle]

a Caroline's office is _____ the lift.
b The lift is _____ the kitchen.
c The kitchen is _____ the lift and Karl's office.
d Julie's office is _____.

**In Company in action**

**8** Antonio arrives at BetterDrinks' office building. Watch video B2. Which room from 7 is the meeting room?

Room A ☐    Room B ☐    Room C ☐

**9** Watch video B2 again and answer the questions.

a Why is Karl late?
  i   He went to the hotel first.
  ii  There was a problem with his train.
  iii He was talking to Julie.
b Where is the BetterDrinks office?
  i   On the third floor.
  ii  Next to the lift.
  iii Across the street.
c Why does Karl want to speak to Julie before the meeting?
  i   The tea for the meeting is not delicious.
  ii  There's a big problem in Taiwan.
  iii He did not bring the Bubble tea.

**10** With a partner, take turns to ask where places are.

Speaker A: Look at page 86.    Speaker B: Look at page 82.

Evaluate your performance using the **Reviewing objectives** box on page 85.

**B IT'S VERY CLOSE**

# 05

## I'm here to see Jo

> *All lasting business is built on friendship.*
>
> Alfred A. Montapert, writer
>
> **Circle the correct answer.**
> Alfred A. Montapert thinks friendship *is / isn't* important for business.

### Learning objectives: Unit 5

**Business communication skills** Making small talk; Roleplay: Visiting an office
**Reading** Emails; Office floor plans
**Listening** Conversations with small talk; Showing someone around the office
**Vocabulary** Small talk; Job titles; Departments
**Grammar** Prepositions: *in, on, opposite, next to*
**Phrase bank** Arranging a visit; Visiting a company

### Writing tips

To join two contrasting sentences, you can use *but*.

*I am out of the office from Monday to Wednesday, but I can meet on Thursday or Friday.*

*The train was comfortable, but it was late.*

*The hotel is quiet, but it's very expensive.*

Remember to use a comma (,) before *but*.

## Arranging a meeting

**1** Read the text and circle the correct answer.

a The text is *a notice / an email*.
b The text is about planning a *holiday / meeting*.

---

**To:** Alex Kantar
**From:** Jo Schmitt
**Subject:** Planning meeting
**Date:** 24 November

Dear Alex,

Good to talk to you on the phone yesterday. I like your plan for marketing our hotel brand through Facebook and Twitter. You have some great ideas. We don't use social media at the moment.

We need to meet soon and write a marketing plan. Next week is good for me. Can you meet on Thursday or Friday morning? I can meet in Paris – or is Frankfurt better? My mobile number is 07432 869 681 if you need to contact me.

I look forward to meeting you soon.

Best wishes,

Jo

Jo Schmitt
Marketing Manager
EuroClass Hotels
Frankfurt

---

**2** Read the email again and answer the following questions.

a What is Jo's job? _____
b Why does she want to meet Alex? _____
c How do they want to market their hotel brand? _____
d When do they plan to meet? _____

**3** Read Alex's reply and complete the smartphone reminder.

---

**To:** Jo Schmitt
**From:** Alex Kantar
**Subject:** Planning meeting
**Date:** 24 November

Dear Jo,

Thank you very much for your email. It's great you like my idea to use social media in our next marketing campaign. I am out of the office next Thursday, but I can meet on Friday (1st December). Frankfurt is good for me – I can work on the train from Paris. About one o'clock?

I look forward to meeting you on Friday.

Best wishes,

Alex

Alex Kantar
Marketing Assistant
EuroClass Hotels
Paris

---

**Reminders**

Meeting
Alex Kantar

Day of meeting
a

Date
b

Time
c

Place
d

**BUSINESS COMMUNICATION**

## Meeting visitors 🎧 💬

**1** 🔊 **1.46** Listen to the conversation and decide if these statements are true (T) or false (F).

a  Alex is a visitor to the head office of EuroClass Hotels.  T / F
b  Alex wants to see Jo.  T / F
c  Jo is not in the office.  T / F

**2** 🔊 **1.46** Complete the sentences using the words in the box. Then listen again and check your answers.

| just   moment   seat   see   welcome |

a  _____ to EuroClass Hotels.
b  I'm here to _____ Jo.
c  _____ a moment, please.
d  She'll be here in a _____.
e  Please take a _____.

> 💬 **Natural language: small talk**
>
> To ask about business/a person's work, we can say:
> *How's business?*
> *How's work?*
> Possible answers:
> *Good, thanks.*
> *It's going really well.*
> *Not so good, actually.*

**3** Work with a partner and take turns being A and B.

**A  Receptionist**                                         **Visiting colleague  B**

1  Welcome your visitor to EuroClass hotels

   2  Say your name and that you're here to see (say a name)

3  Ask them to wait a moment and take a seat

   4  Say thank you

**4** 🔊 **1.47** Listen to the conversation and circle the correct answer.

a  Jo and Alex are *good friends / meeting for the first time*.
b  Jo and Alex talk about *Alex's journey / their meeting*.
c  It is Alex's *first visit to Frankfurt / second visit to Frankfurt*.
d  Alex thinks the office is *new / great*.
e  Jo offers Alex *tea / coffee*.

**5** 🔊 **1.47** Listen again and tick (✓) the phrases you hear.

a  How are you?  ☐
b  What's your name?  ☐
c  How was your journey?  ☐
d  Where are you from?  ☐
e  Is this your first visit here?  ☐
f  Can I get you a coffee?  ☐

> **❓ QUESTION TIME**
>
> **Match the answers to the questions.**
>
> a  How are you?
> b  Is this your first visit here?
> c  Can I get you a coffee?
> d  How was your journey?
>
> I'm okay, thank you. *a*
> It was very good, thanks. __
> It was okay, but the train was late. __
> No, I know the city very well, actually. __
> No, thanks, I'm fine. __
> Oh, I'd love one, thank you. __
>
> Sorry, I don't drink coffee. __
> Very well, thanks. __
> Yes, it is. __
> Yes, please, black no sugar. __
> Yes, please, that would be lovely. __

**6** Work with a partner. Take turns to ask and answer questions using the small talk phrases in 5.

> How was your journey?    It was very good, thanks.

**05 I'M HERE TO SEE JO**

## This is my office

**1** 🎧 1.48 Listen and match the people to their jobs.

a  Alex
b  Angela
c  Ronald
d  Roberta

1  Head of finance
2  Marketing assistant, EuroClass Hotels Paris
3  Head of HR
4  Department administrator

**2** 1.48 Listen again and complete the sentences using the words in the box.

| It's   She's   There's   This is |

a  _____ Head of HR.
b  _____ a small kitchen for staff to use.
c  _____ just through the main doors.
d  _____ my office.

**3** Look at the office building and complete the sentences using the prepositions in the box. Use the pictures on the left to help you.

| in   next to   on   opposite |

a  The open-plan office is _____ the first floor.
b  The reception desk is _____ the main entrance.
c  The customers are _____ Reception.
d  The toilet is _____ the seating area.

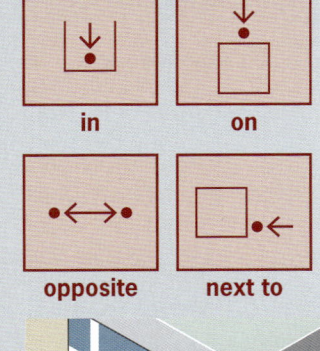

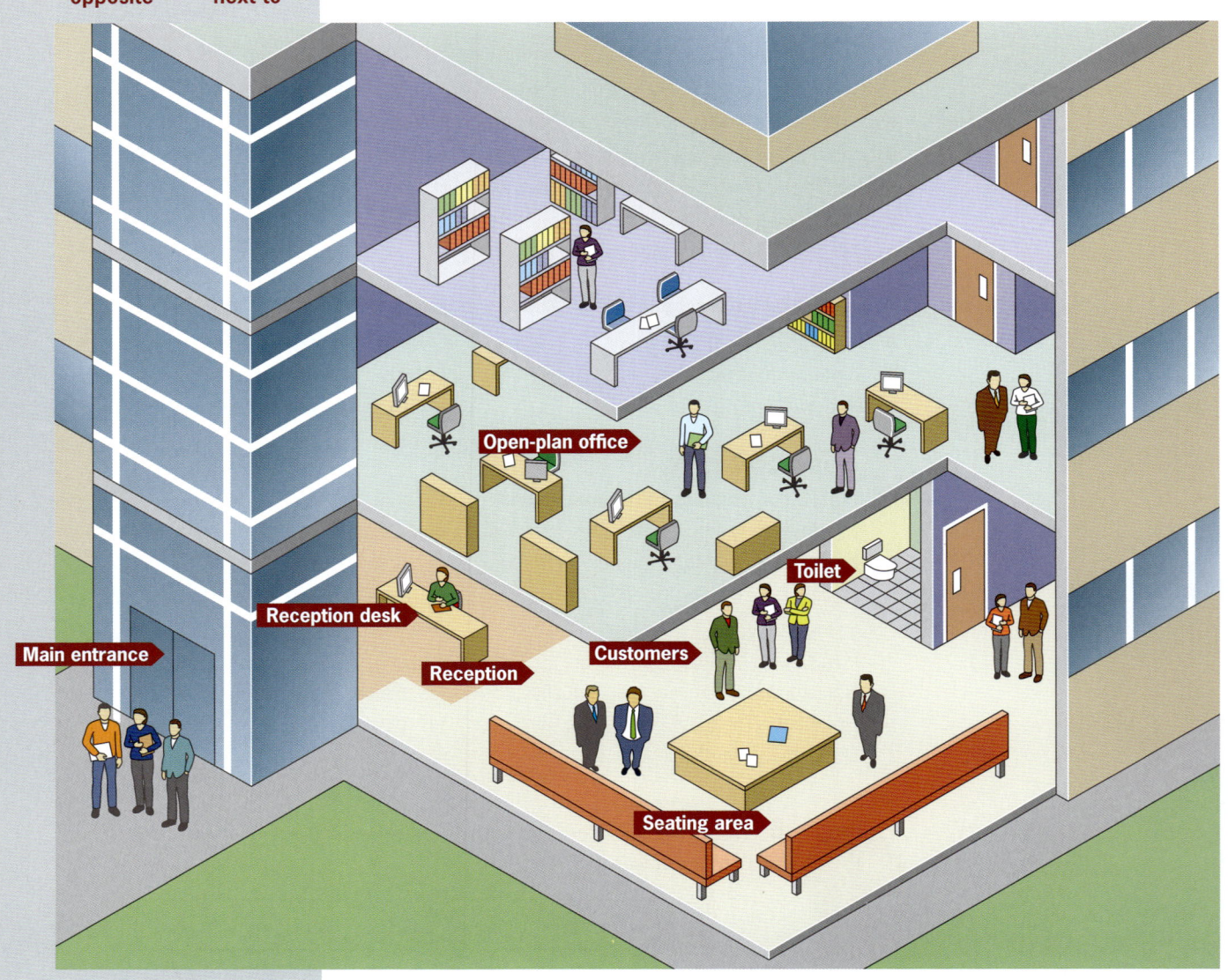

in

on

opposite

next to

Main entrance

Reception desk

Reception

Open-plan office

Customers

Toilet

Seating area

05 I'M HERE TO SEE JO

## BUSINESS COMMUNICATION

**EuroClass Hotels head office**
Ground floor

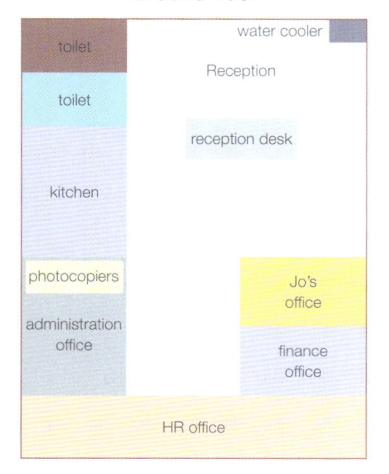

[Floor plan: Ground floor showing toilet, toilet, kitchen, photocopiers, administration office, HR office, water cooler, Reception, reception desk, Jo's office, finance office]

First floor

[Floor plan: First floor showing meeting room 2, coffee area, meeting room 1, Corridor, and spaces labelled A, B, C]

**4** Look at the floor plan for EuroClass Hotels head office and complete the sentences using the prepositions in the box.

in   next to   on   opposite

a Reception is _____ the ground floor.
b There is a water cooler _____ Reception.
c The finance office is _____ Jo's office.
d The administration office is _____ the finance office.

**5** Look at the ground and first floor plans. Complete the sentences.

a There is a _____ area on the first floor.
b The _____ are in the administration office.
c There aren't any toilets on the _____ floor.
d _____ office is next to the finance office.
e There are two _____ rooms on the first floor.
f The _____ are next to the kitchen.

**6** 🔊 1.49 Listen and complete A, B and C on the first floor plan.

**7** Work with a partner. Use the floor plans and take turns to say where the offices are.

> The marketing office is on the first floor. It's next to …

- The administration office
- Meeting room 2
- The finance office
- The marketing office

**8** Work with a partner. Write a conversation between a host and a visitor using the instructions below.

| A | Host | Visitor | B |
|---|---|---|---|

**1** Welcome your visitor and introduce yourself
*Welcome to (company name). I'm …*

**2** Introduce yourself *Pleased to meet you. I'm …*

**3** Ask your visitor about their journey

**4** Say it was good/bad

**5** Ask if it is their first visit

**6** Say yes/no

**7** Offer your visitor a tea or coffee

**8** Say which one

**9** Offer to show them around

**10** Say yes

**11** Introduce them to your colleagues

**12** Ask a question

**9** Work with a new partner. Take turns to play the host and the visitor. Follow the instructions in 8.

05 I'M HERE TO SEE JO

# 05 I'm here to see Jo

### Vocabulary

## Small talk

**1** Put the words in the correct order to make phrases a receptionist might use.

a  a just please moment
   _____.

b  take please seat a
   _____.

c  your can take I name
   _____?

d  is you Stefan see here to
   _____.

**2** Put the sentences in the correct order to make a conversation.

a  I'm here to see … ___
b  Thank you. ___
c  Good morning. My name is … ___
d  I'll see if she's in her office. ___
e  Just a moment, please. ___
f  How can I help you? ___

**3** Match the sentence beginnings (1–4) to the endings (a–d) to make small talk questions.

1  How was         a  you?
2  Is this         b  get you a coffee?
3  Can I           c  your journey?
4  How are         d  your first visit?

**4** Match the answers below to the questions in 3.

a  No, it isn't. ☐
b  I'm good, thank you. ☐
c  Yes please, that would be lovely. ☐
d  It was very good, thanks. ☐

**5** (Circle) the *two* correct answers to the small talk questions.

a  How was your journey?
   *It was good, thanks. / Not bad, thank you. / And you?*
b  Are you new to the company?
   *Yes, I started last month. / Great, thank you. / No, I'm not.*
c  Is this your first visit here?
   *That would be lovely. / No, it isn't. / Yes, it's the first time.*

## Job titles

**6** Put the words in the correct order to make job titles.

a  administrator department  _____
b  finance of head  _____
c  resources manager human  _____

### Grammar

## Prepositions: *in/on*

**1** Write the correct preposition, *in* or *on*.

a  _____ London
b  _____ the first floor
c  _____ the train
d  _____ the phone
e  _____ my email
f  _____ my office

**2** Complete the questions using the words in the box.

| are | can | do | is | was |

a  _____ I take your name?
b  Where _____ the toilets?
c  How _____ your journey?
d  _____ this your first visit here?
e  _____ you have any questions?

### Pronunciation

## Sentence stress

**1** <u>Underline</u> the stressed words and syllables in the sentences.
*I can <u>meet</u> on <u>Fri</u>day.*

a  I can meet in Paris.
b  When can we meet?
c  I'm here to see Jo.
d  How was your journey?
e  Is this your first visit here?
f  That would be lovely.
g  This is my office.

**2** 🔊 **1.50** Listen and check your answers.

# LANGUAGE LINKS

## Phrase bank:

Put these sentences in the correct order to make two conversations.

**Arranging a visit:**

a   Sure. How about Friday?   ☐
b   Is next week okay?   ☐
c   We need to meet soon.   ☐
d   Friday is good for me.   ☐

**Visiting a company:**

a   She'll be here in a moment.   ☐
b   I'm here to see Jo.   ☐
c   Just a moment, please.   ☐
d   Hi, Jo, Alex is here to see you.   ☐
e   Thank you.   ☐

## Using language

(Circle) the *two* correct questions for each use of language.

a   Making small talk
    *How was your journey? / Can I help you? / Is this your first visit?*

b   Asking for information
    *Would you like a coffee? / Where's your office? / Can I take your name?*

c   Making a plan
    *Can you meet on Tuesday? / Is one o'clock good for you? / How's business?*

## Writing

### Emails

Complete the email using the words in the box.

but   can   good   office   thank you

Dear Marc,

(a) _____ very much for your email. It's always good to meet. I am out of the (b) _____ next Wednesday, (c) _____ I can meet on Thursday (10th July). Milan is (d) _____ for me, too – I (e) _____ work on the train from Zurich.

I look forward to meeting you on Thursday.

Best wishes,

Fiona

## Reviewing objectives

Tick (✓) the statements which are true for you.

I can arrange a meeting   ☐
I can welcome visitors and make small talk.   ☐
I can say where things are in an office.   ☐

## My notes from Unit 05

# 06 Let's make a start

*I don't do meetings.*

Karl Lagerfeld, fashion designer

Circle the correct option.

Karl Lagerfeld *likes / doesn't like* meetings.

**Learning objectives: Unit 6**

**Business communication skills** Taking part in meetings; Fluency: Discussing types of advertising
**Reading** Meeting agenda; Blog post
**Listening** Introduction to a meeting; Conversation about meetings; Marketing meeting
**Vocabulary** Meeting words and phrases
**Grammar** Frequency words, verbs, nouns and time phrases; Questions with *How often/Do you*
**Phrase Bank** Useful phrases for meetings
**In Company interviews** Units 5–6

## Meetings

**1** 2.01 Listen to the introduction to a meeting and circle the correct number of items the group will talk about.

1   2   3   4

**2** 2.01 Listen again and complete the agenda.

**AGENDA**

Chair:      Carol Taylor
Minutes:    (a) _____
Item 1:     (b) _____ in Japan
Item 2:     Changes to laws in (c) _____
Item 3:     Problems in other countries

**Items:**
The first item = topic 1
The second item = topic 2
The third item = topic 3
The fourth item = topic 4
Let's go onto the first item = let's talk about topic 1

**3** Label each picture with a word in the box.

a discussion    a meeting    problems    the agenda    the minutes    solutions

A _____  B _____  C _____  D _____  E _____  F _____

**4** Match each word in 3 to the verbs they are often used with. Some words can be used more than once.

| chair | *a meeting* | discuss | _____ | lead | _____ |
|---|---|---|---|---|---|
| read | _____ | find | _____ | take | _____ |

**5** 2.02 Listen to Jan and Claudia talking about meetings in their company and match each word in A to the time periods in B.

A                B
always           I don't do it
sometimes        about three or four times a week
usually          every day
never            about twice a week

**6** Place the words in the box on the scale.

always   never   often   sometimes   usually

Does not happen ————————————————→ Happens all the time

BUSINESS COMMUNICATION

### Writing tips

When talking about time, we must be careful where we put the time phrase. Time phrases usually go in the middle of the sentence:

*I sometimes take minutes.*

Some time phrases go at the end of the sentence:

*We have a meeting every day.*

Decide where to put the time phrase in these examples.

a   I chair meetings. (never)
b   I have meetings. (twice a week)
c   I take the minutes. (always)
d   I have a meeting. (every day)

**7** Delete the incorrect word(s) in each sentence. Use the examples in the Writing tips to help you.

a   I always chair the meeting always.
b   I chair every day a meeting every day.
c   I usually read the agenda usually.
d   I four times a week write the agenda four times a week.
e   I sometimes take the minutes often.

**8** 2.02 Listen to Jan and Claudia again and complete the conversation.

**Claudia:** Right, I have another meeting. So many meetings!
**Jan:** Really, that many? How (a) _____ do you have meetings?
**Claudia:** Oh, it's not too bad, actually. Only sometimes, about twice a week. What about you?
**Jan:** I'm always in a meeting. We have meetings every day, actually. I'm writing the agenda for tomorrow now. Do you (b) _____ read the agenda at the beginning?
**Claudia:** Sometimes. We don't (c) _____ use an agenda, but I always take the minutes, at every meeting. (d) _____ you take the minutes?
**Jan:** No, I don't do that. I never take the minutes. I (e) _____ chair the meeting, about three or four times a week. How (f) _____ do you chair meetings?
**Claudia:** Oh, sometimes, probably about once a month. Anyway, sorry, I need to go, my other meeting's starting.

### ❓ QUESTION TIME
**Write the missing words to complete the questions.**

| | | |
|---|---|---|
| How often | _____ | chair meetings? |
| | | read the agenda? |
| | | take minutes? |
| Do you | _____ /sometimes/ _____ | chair meetings? |
| | | read the agenda? |
| | | take minutes? |

**9** Match each question (a–e) to an answer (1–5).

a   How often do you chair meetings?
b   Do you always read the agenda?
c   How often do you take minutes?
d   Do you sometimes discuss problems?
e   How often do you have meetings?

1   We sometimes read the agenda but not always.
2   I sometimes take minutes, about twice a month.
3   We have a meeting every day.
4   I never chair meetings.
5   We always discuss problems but we never find solutions.

**10** Write sentences about meetings in your company using the information in the box.

| book a meeting room | chair the meeting | read the agenda |
| read the minutes | take minutes | write the agenda |

a   We always …
b   We never …
c   We sometimes …
d   We usually …

**11** Work with a partner and ask about meetings in their company.

> How often do you read the agenda?

> We always read the agenda.

**06 LET'S MAKE A START**

## Taking part in meetings

**1** Read the agenda and tick (✓) the correct answer.

The meeting takes place in:
a  The finance department ☐
b  The marketing department ☐
c  The human resources department ☐

Chair: Jan Carsten
Minutes: Monika Stabrawa
Item 1: Finalise the product launch date
Item 2: Discuss the advertising strategy
Item 3: Discuss celebrity sponsorship options

**2** 2.03 Listen to the meeting and underline the item from the agenda in 1 the people are discussing.

**3** 2.03 Listen again and decide if these statements are true (T) or false (F).
a  Everyone likes Internet advertising.   T / F
b  TV and Internet advertising are expensive.   T / F
c  Not all participants think a mixed advertising strategy is a good idea.   T / F
d  The group makes a final decision on advertising.   T / F

**4** 2.03 Complete the phrases using the words in the box. Listen again and check your answers.

but   good   jump   just   opinion   think   understand   what

a  I _____, but …
b  Okay, _____ …
c  Could I _____ in here?
d  Could I _____ say …
e  I see _____ you mean.
f  That's a _____ point.
g  In my _____, …
h  I _____ we should …

**5** Match each of the phrases in 4 to their use.

| Giving your opinion | Interrupting someone |
|---|---|
| I think _____ | _____ |
| _____ | _____ |

| Agreeing with someone | Disagreeing with someone |
|---|---|
| _____ | _____ |
| _____ | _____ |

---

### 💬 Natural language

We hear a lot of phrases in meetings. The best thing is to keep it simple.

To give an opinion, we can simply say:
*I think …* or
*I guess …*

💬 *I guess we need to increase staff.*

To disagree, a common simple phrase is:
*Yes, but …*

💬 *I think we need to increase staff.*
💬 *Yes, but it would cost too much.*

# BUSINESS COMMUNICATION

## Blog post 📖 ✏️ 💬

**1** Read the blog post about different types of advertising and make notes in the table using information from the blog.

> So, let's look at the good and bad points of different types of advertising.
>
> First, let's talk about TV. A lot of people watch TV, and TV adverts can become popular, but they are expensive and take a long time to make.
>
> Okay, let's look at radio. Radio adverts are cheap, but not many people listen to the radio, and not all popular radio stations have adverts.
>
> Let's talk about the Internet now. Internet adverts are cheap to make and lots of people use the Internet, but people don't always read the adverts.
>
> Finally, let's look at newspapers and magazines. These ads are cheap, but not so many people read newspapers and magazines these days.
>
> So, all types of advertising have good and bad points.

|  | Good points | Bad points |
|---|---|---|
| **TV** |  |  |
| **Internet** |  |  |
| **Radio** |  |  |
| **Newspapers/Magazines** |  |  |

**2** Complete these blog comments about advertising using some of the phrases in the box.

> Could I jump in here    Could I just say    I see what you mean    ~~I think~~
> I understand, but    Okay, but    That's a good point

- *I think* TV is the best type of advertising.
  _____

- In my opinion, radio is a good form of advertising.
  _____ not many people listen to the radio.

- I guess Internet advertising is bad because people don't read the ads.
  _____ the Internet is very popular.

**In Company interviews Units 5–6**

**3** Have a meeting in a group of four. Discuss and choose the best type of advertising.

- I think a lot of people watch TV.
- I understand, but it's expensive.

**06 LET'S MAKE A START**

# 06 Let's make a start

## Vocabulary

### Meetings

**1** Use the letters to help you complete the words in each box.

| ch___r/l___d | a meeting / a discussion |
| r___a___ | an agenda |
| t___k___ | the minutes |
| d___s___ss/f___n | solutions / problems |

**2** Match the words in the box to the correct stress pattern.

| agenda | discussion | meeting |
| minutes | problems | solutions |

•  •           •  •  •
meeting

## Grammar

### Frequency words, verbs, nouns and time phrases

**1** Write sentences about your company using the ideas in the box.

| Frequency words | Verbs | Nouns | Time phrases |
|---|---|---|---|
| always | chair | solutions | every day |
| sometimes | read | the agenda | four times a |
| usually | find | problems | week |
| never | lead | (a) discussion(s) | once a week |
| | take | (a) meeting(s) | |
| | discuss | the minutes | |

a  *I never chair meetings./I chair meetings every day.*
b  _____
c  _____
d  _____
e  _____

## Questions with How often/Do you

**2** Write questions using the information below.

a  often / have meetings?
   *How often do you have meetings?*

b  always / read agenda?
   _____

c  usually / take the minutes?
   _____

d  sometimes / lead meetings?
   _____

e  often / read the minutes?
   _____

f  always / chair the meeting?
   _____

### Using language

Match each sentence to a definition.

a  I always chair meetings.
b  I sometimes take the minutes.
c  We usually read the agenda.
d  We always discuss problems.
e  We never find solutions.
f  We usually go onto new items.

1  It happens all the time.           ___  ___
2  It happens a lot.                  ___  ___
3  It happens, but not all the time.  ___
4  It doesn't happen.                 ___

# LANGUAGE LINKS

## Pronunciation

### Frequency word stress

1 <u>Underline</u> the stressed words in these questions.
a <u>How</u> <u>often</u> do you <u>read</u> the <u>agenda</u>?
b Do you always read the minutes?
c Do you usually chair the meeting?
d How often do you lead meetings?
e How often do you have meetings?

2 🔊 2.04 Listen and check your answers.

3 🔊 2.04 Listen again and repeat each question.

### Phrase bank: Useful phrases for meetings

Use the phrases in the box to complete the conversation. There is more than one possible phrase for some gaps.

| Could I just say | ~~In my opinion~~ |
| I understand, but | I see what you mean | I think |
| Okay, but | That's a good point |

| (give opinion) *In my opinion*, we need to increase prices. | (disagree) (a) _____ we'd lose customers. |
| (agree) (b) _____. How can we increase profits then? | (interrupt) (c) _____ we can save costs in the manufacturing process. |
| (disagree) (d) _____ how do we cut costs? | (agree) (e) _____. |

## Writing

### Agendas

Read the agenda and complete the information.

**Agenda**
Chair: Barbara Bradford
Minutes: Chris Taylor
Item 1: Sales figures for last year
Item 2: Forecast for next year
Item 3: The staff summer party

The chair of the (a) _____ is Barbara Bradford, and Chris Taylor will (b) _____ the minutes. There are three (c) _____ on the agenda. The (d) _____ item is the sales figures for (e) _____ year. The second (f) _____ is the forecast for next (g) _____, and the (h) _____ (and perhaps most important) item is the summer party for the (i) _____.

### Reviewing objectives

Tick (✓) the statements which are true for you.

I can agree, disagree, give my opinion and interrupt in meetings. ☐
I can say how often I do things. ☐
I can ask other people how often they do things. ☐
I can understand words and phrases in a meeting. ☐

# My notes from Unit 06

## SURVIVAL SCENARIO C

**Learning objectives:
Workplace Scenario C**

**Business communication skills**
Asking for a favour;
Responding to requests for a favour; Roleplay: Making and responding to requests for a favour
**Reading** Business article: How to ask for a favour
**In Company in action**
C1: I know you're busy but …;
C2: There's just one more thing

# Don't mention it

**1** Read the sentence and (circle) the correct answer.

People ask for favours when they *need / don't need* your help.

**2** Match each request for a favour to a photo.

a Can I borrow your pen?
b Can I use your phone?
c Can you lend me some money?
d Can I have some paper?

**3** Caroline is the Financial Director of BetterDrinks UK. She is in her office. Watch video C1 and (circle) the correct answer.

a Caroline is very *busy / tired* at the moment.
b Julie asks Caroline for a *favour / job*.
c Antonio is here to try *black tea / Bubble tea*.
d Julie asks Caroline to go to the *kitchen / supplier*.
e Caroline *helps / doesn't help* Julie.

**4** Complete Julie's sentences with the words in the box. Watch video C1 again to check your answers.

| ask | busy | help | so | something | soon |

a I need to _____ you for a favour.
b I know you're _____, but …
c I really need your _____.
d Can you do _____ for me?
e We need it as _____ as possible.
f Thank you _____ much.

48  C DON'T MENTION IT

SURVIVAL SCENARIO

**5** Read the web article and match the sentences below to the 'Top tips'.

a  I'll get to the point. Can I use your laptop? `3`
b  Are you busy? I want to ask you something. ☐
c  Let me explain what the problem is. ☐
d  Thank you very much for your help. ☐

### TOP TIPS: How to ask for a favour

In business, we often need to ask people for favours, but sometimes it can be difficult. Here are some top tips on how to ask for a favour and get what you need.

**1** Choose the right time. Don't ask someone for a favour when the other person is busy or stressed.

**2** Explain the problem. Tell the other person why you need the favour.

**3** Get to the point. Don't waste time or talk for too long before you ask for the favour.

**4** Be polite. Remember to say please and thank you.

**6** Work with a partner. Put the phrases below in the correct column.

a  I need to
b  Can you/I ?
c  Could you ?
d  ... is that okay?
e  Okay, I'll do that.
f  That's fine.
g  The problem is
h  Sure. No problem.
i  All right.

| Asking for a favour | Agreeing to do a favour |
| --- | --- |
|  |  |

**7** Use the phrases in 6 to complete the conversation. Then practise the conversation with a partner.

A

1  *I need to* make a phone call.

3  _____ I don't have my phone.

5  _____ use your phone?

7  Head office. I won't be long. _____

B

2  Okay.

4  Okay.

6  _____. Who are you calling?

8  _____. Here's the phone.

In Company in action

**8** Later the same day, Karl talks to Caroline. Watch video C2 and look at the table in 6. <u>Underline</u> the phrases you hear.

**9** Who says these phrases? Write *K* (Karl) or *C* (Caroline). Watch video C2 again to check your answers.

a  I just want to say thank you. ____
b  Don't mention it. ____
c  It's fine, really. ____
d  Don't worry about it. ____
e  ... there's just one more thing. ____
f  I'm sorry to trouble you. ____

**10** Work with a partner. Practise asking for a favour and responding.

Speaker A: Look at page 87.    Speaker B: Look at page 88.

Evaluate your performance using the **Reviewing objectives** box on page 84.

C  DON'T MENTION IT

# 07

*Change is the law of life and those who look only to the past or present are certain to miss the future.*

John F. Kennedy, former President of the United States

**Circle** the correct option.
John F. Kennedy thinks change is *important* / *unimportant*.

### Learning objectives: Unit 7

**Business communication skills**
Talking about changes in technology; Fluency: Talking about your life and career
**Reading** Article about changing technology
**Listening** The life of a business speaker; *-ed* pronunciation
**Vocabulary** Adjectives and opposites
**Grammar** Past Simple
**Phrase bank** Talking about technology and communication

# Business on the move

## Technology and communication

**1** Match the adjectives (a–h) to their opposites (1–8).

| a | small | 1 | cheap | e | new | 5 | unimportant |
| b | expensive | 2 | big | f | happy | 6 | old |
| c | fast | 3 | unpopular | g | heavy | 7 | light |
| d | popular | 4 | slow | h | important | 8 | unhappy |

**2** Match the words in the box to the pictures (a–f).

| app | cloud computing | hands-free | smartphone | tablet | Wi-Fi |

**3** Circle the ways you communicate.
a I use smartphones to *make phone calls / check my emails / write PowerPoint presentations*.
b I send emails with my *laptop / smartphone / tablet*.
c I don't use *a tablet / cloud computing / hands-free*.
d I use apps to *talk to customers / download music / learn English*.

**4** Work in groups. Say which communication technologies you use.

I use (my) ... to send emails.
to Skype.
to write Word documents.
to access my documents when travelling.

**5** 2.05 The Past Simple tense of *be* is *was/were*. Listen to the speaker and tick (✓) the verbs you hear.

are ☐   do ☐   is ☐   send ☐   use ☐   was ☐   were ☐

**6** 2.05 Complete the table with *was/were*. Listen again and check your answers.

|  | The Present Simple of *be* | The Past Simple of *be* |
|---|---|---|
| I | am | |
| you | are | were |
| he/she/it | is | |
| we | are | were |
| you | are | were |
| they | are | |

## BUSINESS COMMUNICATION

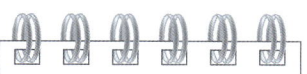

### Writing tips

When we use a time phrase for the present or past, we often put it at the beginning of a sentence.

When we do that, we usually use a comma after it.

*Today, business people have smartphones.*

*Around the year 2000, laptops were popular.*

**7** Complete the text using *was/were* or *is/are*.

#### The history of business communication

Communication in business (a) _____ easier today than it (b) _____ 30 years ago. In the 1980s, mobile phones (c) _____ big and heavy; today, of course, they (d) _____ small and light. Then they (e) _____ expensive, but today they (f) _____ cheap. Also, cloud computing (g) _____ an important development – this means people can access their work 'on the move' when they (h) _____ away from the office.

### QUESTION TIME

Write questions for sentences a–d:

a It was cheap. *Was it cheap?*
b It was expensive. _____
c They were popular. _____
d You were happy. _____

**8** Choose adjectives to describe your phones. Write these in the table.

| big   cheap   expensive   fast   heavy   light   new   old   small   slow |

| Your first phone | Your present phone |
|---|---|
|  |  |

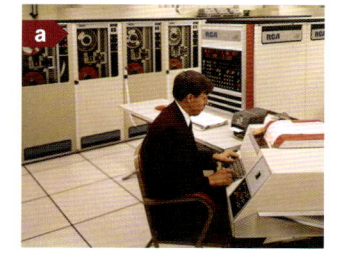

**9** Complete the sentences using adjectives from 8.

a My first smartphone was _____.
b It was _____.
c Now, I have a _____ smartphone.
d It is _____.

**10** Work with a partner. Make questions using the information in 9.

> Was your first phone expensive?

> What phone do you have now?

**11** Read the text and write a time phrase below the photos (a–d).

In the 1960s, computers were big and slow. They were also expensive, so they were not popular. Twenty years later, in the 1980s, computers were not very small but they were quite fast. At that time, laptops were popular for small and big businesses. Around the year 2000, laptops were popular for everyone. Today, business people have smartphones. These are very small, fast, they have many functions and applications, and they are not very expensive. Most business-to-business (B2B) communication today is mobile, using phone and email.

**12** Complete the sentences using information from the text and the words in the box.

| 1960s   computers   email   fast   laptops   smartphone |

a Computers were big and slow in the _____. Today, they are _____.
b In the 1960s, _____ were not popular, but _____ were popular in 2000.
c Today, business people communicate by _____ and _____.

**13** Work with a partner. Take turns to make sentences using the following conformation.

| Vocabulary: time phrases | Topic | Verb | Adjective |
|---|---|---|---|
| In the 1960s, In the 1980s, | computers | were | fast / slow |
| Around the year 2000, | laptops |  | expensive / not very expensive |
| Today, Now, | smartphones | are | popular / not popular |

**07 BUSINESS ON THE MOVE**

## The life of a business speaker

**1** 2.06 Listen and circle the correct answer.
a Simon Sinek is a *writer and teacher / leader and manager*.
b He lives in *London / New York*.
c The title of his book is *Why Do We Talk? / Start With Why*.

**2** Complete the text using the correct form of the verbs in the box.

ask   be (am/is/are)   introduce   live   move   start   study   work

Simon Sinek (a) _____ a writer and teacher in business and leadership. When he was young he (b) _____ in London, South Africa and Hong Kong. Then he (c) _____ to the USA. He now lives in New York. He (d) _____ at City University in London, and now teaches business at Columbia University in New York. Simon Sinek (e) _____ the idea of the 'golden circle'. This (f) _____ with the question 'Why?' After that it (g) _____ the question 'How?', and finally asks the question 'What?' This is the topic of his book – its title is *Start With Why*. He (h) _____ in the USA, and gives talks and lectures. His talk on Ted.com is very popular, and millions of people watch it every year!

**3** 2.06 Listen again and check.

**4** 2.07 Listen and circle the verb forms you hear.
a is / was
b lives / lived
c move / moved
d studies / studied
e introduce / introduced
f starts / started
g asks / asked
h works / worked

**5** Complete the rules about the Past Simple in English.
- To form the Past Simple of regular verbs, add _____ to the verb. work → worked
- When the verb ends in _____, just add 'd'. live → lived
- When the verb ends in 'y', change the 'y' to _____ and then add 'ed'. study → studied
- The verb *be* is irregular. The past is *was* (singular) and *were* (plural). be → was/were

**6** Complete the table.

| Present Simple | Past Simple |
| --- | --- |
| live | lived |
| listen | |
| start | |
| | showed |
| want | |
| | liked |
| study | |

**7** 2.08 Listen and repeat the Past Simple form of the verbs in this unit.

**8** We pronounce *-ed* in three different ways. Look at the examples and write the words in the correct row of the table.

asked   introduced   ~~liked~~   ~~lived~~   moved   showed   started   studied   ~~wanted~~   worked

| | |
| --- | --- |
| /d/ | lived, |
| /t/ | liked, |
| /ɪd/ | wanted, |

07 BUSINESS ON THE MOVE

**BUSINESS COMMUNICATION**

## Talking about the past

**1** Match the questions (a–e) to the correct answers (1–5).

a Where did you live when you were young?
b What was your favourite subject at school?
c Where did you go to university?
d What did you do after that?
e What do you do now?

1 I studied Mathematics at Leeds University.
2 I lived in Liverpool.
3 I live in London and I work for HSBC.
4 I really liked Maths.
5 I worked for the Bank of Scotland.

**2** 2.09 Listen and check your answers.

**3** Complete the table below.

|  | Positive | Negative | Question |
|---|---|---|---|
| **Present** | I live in London. I work at HSBC. | I don't live in London. I _____ work at HSBC. | Where do you live? Where do you _____? What _____ you do? |
| **Past** | I lived in London. I worked at Barclays. | I _____ _____ in London. I didn't _____ at Barclays. | Where _____ _____ _____? Where did you _____? What _____ you do? |

**4** Write Past Simple questions with *you*, using the information below.

a Where / go to school  _____
b Where / live  _____
c Where / go to university/college  _____
d What / study  _____
e What / do after that  _____

**5** Complete the sentences about your life and career.

a When I was young, I lived in _____. (city/country)
b At school I liked _____ (subject(s)) and I wanted to be a / an _____. (job)
c Then I studied _____ (subject) at _____. (school/university)
d After that I worked for _____. (company)
e Now I live in _____ (place) and I work for _____. (company)

**6** Prepare to interview your partner. Choose 3 or 4 questions from this section, and write one new question.
*Where did you live when you were 18?*

**7** Work with a partner. Take turns to interview each other using your prepared questions.

> What did you do after university?

> I moved to Mexico City.

---

### 💬 Natural language

In conversations, we often use short words and phrases to show interest:
*Okay. Really? Uh huh. I see.*

💬 *I live in Rome now.*
💬 *Really? When did you move there?*
💬 *In 2013.*
💬 *Uh huh. Do you like it?*
💬 *Yes, it's fantastic! It's a beautiful city.*
💬 *Okay … Can I come and visit you?*

07 BUSINESS ON THE MOVE    53

# 07 Business on the move

## Vocabulary

### Adjectives and opposites

**1** Write opposites for the following adjectives.

a old _____   e small _____
b happy _____   f important _____
c cheap _____   g heavy _____
d popular _____   h fast _____

**2** Look at the two pictures and complete the sentences below using the words in the box.

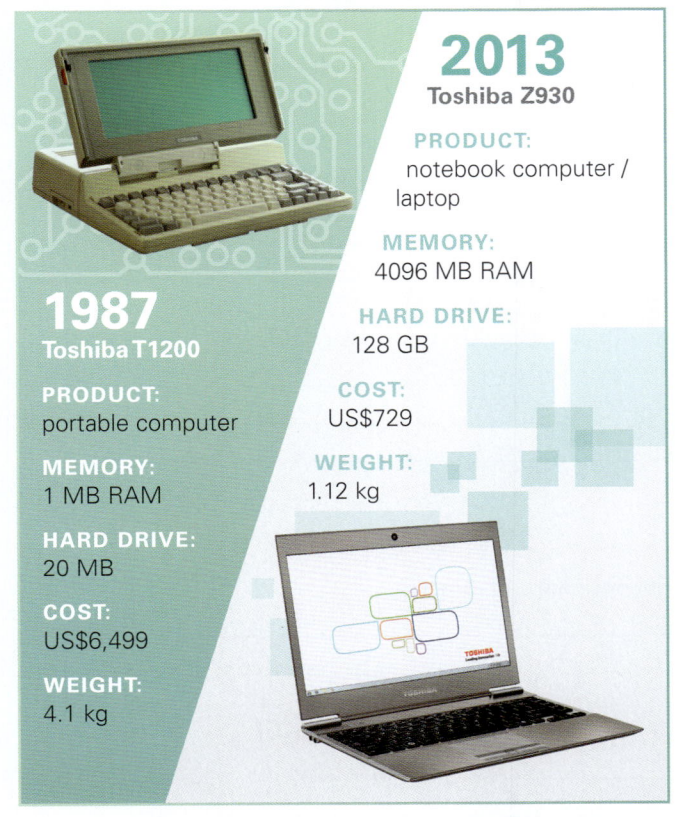

**1987** Toshiba T1200
PRODUCT: portable computer
MEMORY: 1 MB RAM
HARD DRIVE: 20 MB
COST: US$6,499
WEIGHT: 4.1 kg

**2013** Toshiba Z930
PRODUCT: notebook computer / laptop
MEMORY: 4096 MB RAM
HARD DRIVE: 128 GB
COST: US$729
WEIGHT: 1.12 kg

| big | cheap | expensive | heavy | light | small |

a The T1200 has a _____ memory. The Z930 has a _____ memory.
b The 1987 model cost US$6,499, which is _____, but the Z930 is quite _____.
c The old model is 4.1 kg, which is _____, but the Z930 is only 1.12 kg, which is _____.

## Grammar

### Past Simple

**1** Circle the correct verbs.

My first mobile phone (a) *was / were* expensive. It (b) *work / worked* for about three years, then (c) *stop / stopped*. My second mobile (d) *was / were* cheaper, and I (e) *was / were* very happy with it. These two phones (f) *was / were* good then, but they aren't so good now. My new smartphone is beautiful and it can do almost anything!

**2** Put the words in the correct order to make sentences.

a laptops / in the 1980s / slow and expensive / were
_____
b have / today / most people / smartphones
_____
c popular / for businesses / laptops / in the 1980s / were
_____

**3** Write the Past Simple form of the following verbs.

a live _____   f decide _____
b want _____   g introduce _____
c start _____   h show _____
d ask _____   i work _____
e study _____   j use _____

**4** Complete the text using the Past Simple or Present Simple form of the verbs in the box.

| be | live | start | want | work |

When I _was_ a student, I (a) _____ in Berlin. I (b) _____ to go into banking, so I (c) _____ to work for Deutsche Bank. Now I (d) _____ in their HR department.

**5** Complete the questions using *did*, *was* or *were*.

a Where _____ you live when you _____ 15?
b What _____ you study at university?
c Where _____ your first job?
d _____ you happy there?
e What _____ you do after that?
f _____ it an interesting job?

**6** Match the questions (a–f) in 5 with the correct answer (1–6).

1 Not very happy, but it was okay. ____
2 I studied Economics. ____
3 Yes, it was very interesting. ____
4 After that, I worked for a travel company. ____
5 I lived in Madrid. ____
6 My first job was at Elan Engineering. ____

# LANGUAGE LINKS

## Pronunciation

### Past Simple verbs

**1**  2.10 Listen and (circle) the word you hear.
a  I *study / studied* at university.
b  She *is / was* a student at the Beijing Business School.
c  I *work / worked* for Administrators Unlimited.
d  What *do / did* you do?

**2**  2.11 Listen and write the words in the correct row.

| /d/ | *showed,* |
| /t/ | *worked,* |
| /ɪd/ | *started,* |

---

**Phrase bank: Talking about technology and communication**

Put the phrases below in the correct time order.
Today/Now, phones are …
In the 1980s, phones were …
Around the year 2000, …
I use (my tablet) to (write and send documents).

---

## Using language

Which sentences *describe* something, and which ones are about what you do (your *habits*)? Write *D* (describe) or *H* (habit).

a  I use my smartphone to take photos.  ___
b  I take photos with my tablet.  ___
c  My first computer was expensive and slow.  ___
d  Today, I do most of my work on my laptop.  ___
e  I think my car is good, but it was expensive.  ___
f  I am happy with my computer, and it was cheap.  ___

## Writing

### Your life and career

**1**  Write short answers to the following questions.
What was your favourite subject at school?
*Maths*
a  Where did you study?
   _____
b  What did you study at college/university?
   _____
c  What was your first job?
   _____
d  What do you do now?
   _____

**2**  Use the information from 1 to write a paragraph about your life and career. Write two or three sentences. Use *and/but.*

*At school my favourite subject was Maths, but I studied Art at university.*
_____
_____
_____
_____
_____

---

**Reviewing objectives**

Tick (✓) the statements which are true for you.
I can talk about technological changes.  ☐
I can describe past and present situations.  ☐
I can talk about my life and career.  ☐

---

# My notes from Unit 07

# 08 I'd like to talk about …

> There is no such thing as presentation talent – it's called presentation skills.
>
> David JP Phillips, presentation trainer

Circle the correct option.
David JP Phillips thinks people *can / can't* learn to give a presentation.

**Learning objectives: Unit 8**

**Business communication skills**
Giving presentations; Fluency: Talking about changes and results; Roleplay: Giving a sales presentation
**Reading** Email about investment opportunities
**Listening** Presentation about sales results; Question and answer session
**Vocabulary** Describing change
**Grammar** Past Simple irregular verbs; Questions and negatives in the past
**Phrase bank** Useful presentation language
**In Company interviews** Units 7–8

## Presentations

**1** 2.12 Listen to the presentation and circle the correct arrow for each region.

| Europe | | North America | | Asia | |
|---|---|---|---|---|---|
| ↑ | ↓ | ↑ | ↓ | ↑ | ↓ |

**2** 2.12 Listen again and complete the sales figures.

| Region | Last year | This year |
|---|---|---|
| Europe | $13 million | |
| North America | | $13 million |
| Asia | $14 million | |

**3** Place the past tense verbs under the correct arrow. Work with a partner to check your answers.

| increased | went down | rose |
|---|---|---|
| fell | got better | decreased |
| went up | grew | got worse |

| ↑ | ↓ |
|---|---|
| _____ | _____ |
| _____ | _____ |
| _____ | _____ |
| _____ | _____ |
| _____ | _____ |

**4** Match the Present Simple to the Past Simple forms of each verb.

| | Present Simple | Past Simple |
|---|---|---|
| a | increase | rose |
| b | rise | got (better/worse) |
| c | fall | increased |
| d | go (up/down) | grew |
| e | get (better/worse) | decreased |
| f | decrease | fell |
| g | grow | went (up/down) |

**5** Decide if the verbs in 4 are *regular* or *irregular* and circle the correct answer to complete the rule.

Regular verbs:  *increase*  _____
Irregular verbs:  *rise*  _____  _____  _____  _____
Irregular verbs have *different / the same* endings in the Past Simple.

**BUSINESS COMMUNICATION**

> **Natural language**
> There are many ways you can introduce topics in a presentation, but two of the most common are *so* and *now*.
>
> You can use them to:
> introduce a presentation
> *So, I'd like to talk about …*
> to change topic
> *Now, let's move onto …*
> or to end a presentation
> *So, we talked about …*

**6** Use the information in the table and all the words in the box to complete the sentences about *this* year. Try to use each word only once.

| fell | get better/worse | go up/down | grow | increase | rise |

| Country | Last year | This year |
|---|---|---|
| UK | $14 million | $16 million |
| USA | $14 million | $12 million |
| France | $13 million | $14 million |
| Japan | $12 million | $14 million |
| Thailand | $14 million | $4 million |
| Korea | $8 million | $8.5 million |

a  Sales in the UK *increased*_____.
b  Sales in the USA _____.
c  Sales in France _____.
d  Sales in Japan _____.
e  Sales in Thailand _____.
f  Sales in Korea _____.

**7**  2.12 Listen to the presentation again and complete the phrases below using the words in the box.

| first | present | now | recap | finally |

a  Today, I'd like to _____ the sales results for key regions.
b  _____, let me explain results for Europe.
c  _____, I'll outline performance in North America.
d  _____, I'll talk about what happened in Asia.
e  So, to _____, sales in the USA and Asia got better.

**8**  2.13 Listen to the sentences in 7. <u>Underline</u> the stressed words and syllables.

To<u>day</u>, I'd like to pre<u>sent</u> the <u>sales</u> results for <u>key</u> regions.

**Hint!** We usually stress the **important** words in a sentence.

**9** Circle the arrow that is true for your company and then complete the sentence.
a  Profits         ↑↓  Profits in my company _____ last year.
b  Sales           ↑↓  Sales in my company _____ last quarter.
c  Investment      ↑↓  Investment in my company _____ in 2011.
d  Market share    ↑↓  Market share in my company _____ in the last six months.

**10** Use the ideas below to create a short presentation about your company.

1  Today, I'd like to present my company.

2  First, I'll explain profits.

3  <u>Profits</u> in my company …

4  Now I'll outline _____.

5  _____ in my company …

6  Finally, I'll talk about _____.

7  _____ in my company …

8  Okay, to recap …

**11** Work with a partner and give your presentation.

08 I'D LIKE TO TALK ABOUT …

**Writing tips**

Some of the most common ways to end an email are:

a  Yours sincerely, \_\_\_
b  Kind regards/
   Best wishes, \_\_\_
c  Thanks/Best, \_\_\_

Write *F* next to the formal ending, *N* next to the neutral ending and *I* next to the informal ending.

# Q&A

**1** Read the email and circle the correct answer.

Global unemployment *increased / decreased* last month.

---

**Global Economic Performance**

**To:** All Investment Advisors
**From:** Karin Ricards

Dear All,
We expected the global economy to get worse last month, but it got better.
Global inflation fell last month, from 7% to 5%.
Global unemployment also went down, from 8% to 6%.
Investment rose from $17 trillion to $20 trillion.
Overall, the global economy went up and the economic situation got better.
So, we expect investment to go up again this month.
Kind regards,
Karin

---

**2** Use the information in the email and the correct form of the words and phrases in the box to complete the sentences.

> get better   go down   grow   rise

a  Inflation _____ last month.
b  The economic situation _____ last month.
c  Investment _____ last month.
d  The global economy _____ last month.

**3** Complete the table with the verbs in the box.

> didn't   got worse   grow   increase

| Positive verb form | Negative verb form |
|---|---|
| grew | didn't _____ |
| rose | _____ rise |
| _____ | didn't get worse |
| increased | didn't _____ |

**4** Complete these sentences for your country or a country you do business with, using verbs from 1. Try to use a different verb in each gap.

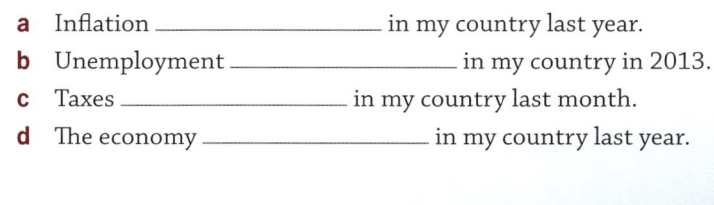

a  Inflation _____ in my country last year.
b  Unemployment _____ in my country in 2013.
c  Taxes _____ in my country last month.
d  The economy _____ in my country last year.

**BUSINESS COMMUNICATION**

**5** Work with a partner and talk about the situations in the box in your country.

inflation    taxes    the economy    unemployment

**6** 2.14 Listen to the Q&A after the presentation and tick (✓) the correct summary.
a Karin says the global economy got better. ☐
b Karin says the global economy got worse. ☐
c Karin does not talk about the global economy. ☐

**7** 2.14 Listen again and complete the conversation.

**Karin:** Okay, so that's all from me. Does anyone have any questions?
**Questioner 1:** Yes, I have a question. (a) _____ investment go up in all countries?
**Karin:** No, not in all countries, but it (b) _____ globally. Any other questions?
**Questioner 2:** I'd like to ask about investor confidence. Did investor confidence (c) _____ worse?
**Karin:** No, it (d) _____ a lot better. People are happy about the global economy. Anyone else?
**Questioner 3:** Yes, what about government debt? (e) _____ the government debt rise?
**Karin:** It's high, but it fell last month.

> **QUESTION TIME**
> Write the missing word to complete the questions.
> _____ profits go up/down?
> _____ investment rise?
> _____ government debt fall?
> _____ unemployment grow?
> _____ the economy get better/worse?

**8** Write questions about the global economy using words and phrases in column 1. Choose a word or phrase which describes change to complete your question.

| 1 | | 2 | 3 |
|---|---|---|---|
| Unemployment | *Did unemployment get worse?* | ↑ | ↓ |
| Taxes | | ↓ | ↑ |
| Inflation | | ↑ | ↓ |
| Government debt | | ↓ | ↑ |
| Investment | | ↑ | ↓ |

*In Company interviews Units 7–8*

**9** Work with a partner.
**Part 1**
Speaker A: ask your questions. Speaker B: answer using the information in column 2.

> Did unemployment get worse?     No, it got better.

**Part 2**
Speaker B: ask your questions. Speaker A: answer using the information in column 3.

> Did unemployment get worse?     Yes, it did.

**10** Work with a partner.
Speaker A: Look at page 83.              Speaker B: Look at page 85.

# 08 I'd like to talk about ...

## Vocabulary

### Describing change

**1** Decide if the words below are in the correct part of the table. If they are wrong, move them to the correct column.

| ↑ | ↓ |
|---|---|
| increased | got better |
| fell | went down |
| went up | grew |
| got worse | decreased |
| rose | |

**2** Complete the sentences using the word in brackets in the Past Simple.

a  Profits *fell* last year. (fall)
b  Costs _____ last year. (rise)
c  Taxes _____ last year. (go down)
d  Government spending _____ last year. (grow)
e  Inflation _____ last year. (go up)
f  Wages _____ last year. (increase)
g  The economy _____ last year. (get better)
h  Sales _____ last year. (decrease)
i  Investment _____ last year. (get worse)

## Grammar

### Past Simple

**1** Complete the table.

| Present | Past Simple | Past Simple negative |
|---|---|---|
| increase | _____ | didn't increase |
| decrease | decreased | didn't _____ decrease |
| get better/worse | got better/worse | didn't _____ better/worse |
| grow | _____ | didn't _____ |
| rise | rose | didn't rise |
| fall | _____ | didn't _____ |
| go up/down | went up/down | didn't _____ go up/down |

**2** Complete the sentences below using the information in the table and the verbs in 1.

| | Last year | This year |
|---|---|---|
| Profits | $2 million | £1.5 million |
| Sales | 500,000 | 700,000 |
| Employees | 2,000 | 1,500 |
| Customers | 15,000 | 17,000 |
| Costs | $2 million | $1.5 million |

a  Profits *fell* _____ this year
b  Sales _____ last year.
c  Employee numbers _____ last year.
d  Customer numbers _____ last year.
e  Costs _____ last year.

**3** Write questions using the information below.

a  profits / fall last year?
   *Did profits fall last year?*
b  sales / go up last month?
   _____?
c  number of employees / rise last year?
   _____?
d  costs / increase last quarter?
   _____?
e  customer numbers / increase last month?
   _____?

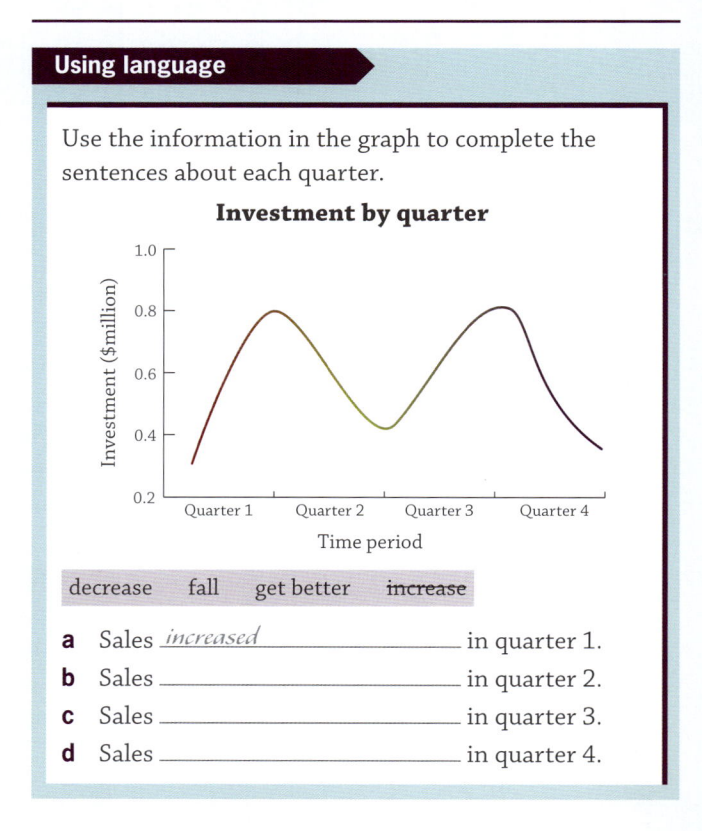

### Using language

Use the information in the graph to complete the sentences about each quarter.

**Investment by quarter**

(Graph showing Investment ($million) from 0.2 to 1.0 across Quarter 1 to Quarter 4)

decrease   fall   get better   ~~increase~~

a  Sales *increased* _____ in quarter 1.
b  Sales _____ in quarter 2.
c  Sales _____ in quarter 3.
d  Sales _____ in quarter 4.

## LANGUAGE LINKS

### Pronunciation

**Word and syllable stress to describe change**

1 <u>Underline</u> the stressed words/syllables in each sentence.
  a Did <u>pro</u>fits <u>fall</u> last year?
  b <u>Pro</u>fits in<u>creased</u> last year.
  c Did costs rise last month?
  d Costs went down last month.
  e Did sales go up last month?
  f Sales went up last year.

2  2.15 Listen and check your answers.

---

**Phrase bank: Useful presentation language**

Put the sentences in the correct order to make a presentation.

  a Finally, I'll talk about new products. We introduced three new products this year.
  b First, I'll talk about profits. The company made $2 million profit this year.
  c To recap, the company made a profit, increased market share and introduced three new products this year.
  d Today, I'd like to present our sales figures.
  e Now, I'll talk about market share. Our market share increased by 5%.

  1 _d_
  2 ___
  3 ___
  4 ___
  5 ___

---

### Writing

**A PowerPoint slide**

Complete the PowerPoint slide with the ideas in the box.

costs / decrease    inflation / increase    investment / rise
market share / go down    profit / grow    unemployment / fall

**KEY MARKET INFORMATION**

  a _Costs decreased last year_
  b _____
  c _____
  d _____
  e _____
  f _____

---

**Reviewing objectives**

Tick (✓) the statements which are true for you.

I can talk about change. ☐
I can talk about the past. ☐
I can give a presentation. ☐
I can ask questions in a presentation. ☐

---

# My notes from Unit 08

## SURVIVAL SCENARIO D

# Click the icon

**Learning objectives:**
**Workplace Scenario D**
**Business communication skills**
Giving instructions and responding to instructions for common office tasks; Roleplay: Giving instructions for sending an email and printing a document
**Reading** Email about a training session
**In Company in action**
D1: It's really easy, I promise;
D2: For an outside line, press 9

**1** Match the computer terms (a–i) to the pictures (1–9).

a icon ____     d log in ____     g type ____
b click ____    e log out ____    h keyboard ____
c password ____ f mouse ____      i cursor ____

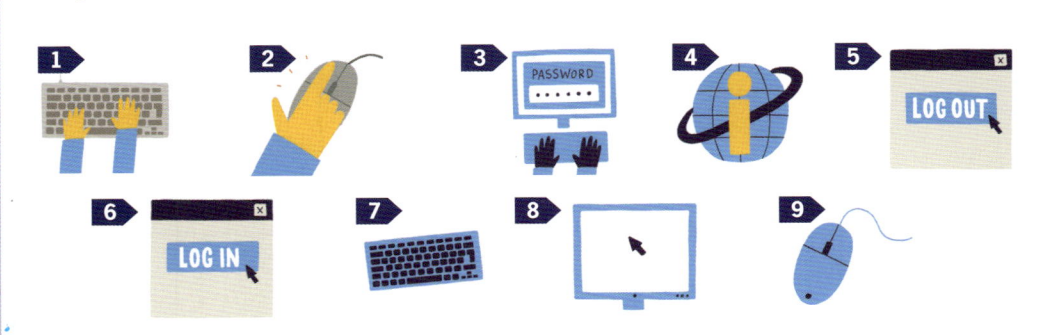

**2** Karl sends Julie an email about a new computer program. Read the email and decide if the statements below are true (T) or false (F).

**From:** Karl Harrison
**To:** Julie Norley
**Date:** 17 May

Hi Julie,

Just to let you know, we have a new computer program for holiday requests. It's called Time Off. We can use it to check available dates for holidays. Caroline knows how to use it, so I asked her to train you. I think the training session will take less than an hour. Please arrange a good time with Caroline as soon as possible.

Thanks,

Karl

**Karl Harrison** | Sales Manager | BetterDrinks UK

a The new program is for making training sessions. T / F
b With Time Off you can check the dates that are available for people to take holidays. T / F
c Caroline designed the computer program. T / F
d The training session will take less than 60 minutes. T / F
e Caroline will arrange the time of the training session with Karl. T / F

**In Company in action**

**3** Caroline shows Julie how to use the new computer program. Watch video D1 and circle the correct answer.

a Caroline thinks the program is *easy / difficult* to use.
b The Time Off icon has a picture of a *calendar / sunbed*.
c Julie thinks the program is *fair / not fair*.

62  D CLICK THE ICON

SURVIVAL SCENARIO

**4** Put the process in the correct order. Watch video D1 again to check your answers.
- a  Click the select button
- b  Click on the icon
- c  Find the calendar
- d  Choose your holiday dates
- e  Close the program
- f  Enter your password

1 _b_   2 ___   3 ___   4 ___   5 ___   6 ___

**5** Work with a partner and decide which phrases show that you understand an instruction ✓, and which phrases show that you need more help ✗.
- a  I've got it.
- b  I don't get it.
- c  Could you repeat that?
- d  I see.
- e  What do you mean?
- f  That makes sense.
- g  I'm confused.
- h  I know what you mean.

**6** Use the words in the box to complete the conversation. Work with a partner and practise the conversation.

decide   put   repeat   see   understand

**A**
1  First, _____ the paper in the photocopier.
3  Choose the size of the paper.
5  Choose the paper size.
7  Then _____ if you want double sided.
9  Do you want the paper on one side or two?

**B**
2  Okay.
4  Sorry, could you _____ that?
6  Okay.
8  Sorry, I don't _____.
10  I _____.

**7** Complete these instructions for making an international phone call using the words in the box.

code   dial   line   number   zero

- a  For an outside _____, press 9.
- b  Then _____ zero zero, for your call to leave the UK.
- c  Next you need to dial the country calling _____.
- d  After that, dial the area code, but take off the first _____.
- e  Next, dial the rest of the phone _____.

In Company in action

**8** Antonio needs to make an international phone call. He asks Julie for help. Watch video D2 and tick (✓) the phrases in 7 that you hear.

**9** Work with a partner. Decide if these statements are true (T) or false (F). Watch video D2 again to check your answers.
- a  Antonio needs to speak to Karl on the phone.   T / F
- b  Antonio knows the number he wants to call.   T / F
- c  You press 6 to get an outside line.   T / F
- d  The number to call out of the UK is 00.   T / F
- e  Antonio doesn't need to use an area code.   T / F

**10** Work with a partner. Practise giving and following instructions.
Speaker A: Look at page 86.   Speaker B: Look at page 88.

Evaluate your performance using the **Reviewing objectives** box on page 83.

D CLICK THE ICON

# 09

*The only place where success comes before work is in the dictionary.*

Vidal Sassoon, hairdresser and businessman

Circle the correct answer.
Vidal Sassoon says you need to work for success. *True / False*

**Learning objectives: Unit 9**

**Business communication skills**
Planning a business event; Roleplay: Organizing food for a business event; Fluency: Giving travel tips to visitors

**Reading** Business invitation

**Listening** Planning business events; Talking about places

**Vocabulary** Opposites; Food; Places

**Grammar** Making suggestions; *some* and *any*

**Phrase bank** Asking for suggestions

# Where should I stay?

## The launch party

**1** Work with a partner. What can a company launch event offer you? Tick (✓) one or more.

You can learn about the new company. ☐
You can meet new business people. ☐
You can do business with the new company. ☐
You can enjoy the food and drink, and talk to people. ☐

**2** 2.16 Sophie and Henry are planning an event. Listen to the conversation and circle the correct options in the invitation.

### ❧ INVITATION ❧

You are invited to the launch of our new training business SE1 Training

| At | On |
|---|---|
| The Regent Hotel, Central Square, London | Friday 10th / 18th / 25th September |
| The Rialto Hotel, London | From 5–7 pm / 6–8 pm / 7–8 pm |
| The Rex Hotel, London | |

Please reply to Sophie@se1training.co.uk

**3** Turn to page 83. Plan a launch event for a new company.

**4** Work with a partner. Ask and answer questions about your event. Write the information in the table.

| Where is the event? | |
|---|---|
| When is it? | |

**5** Match the words (a–h) to their opposites (1–8).

a  expensive         1  worse
b  good              2  light
c  slow              3  small
d  early             4  short
e  better            5  bad
f  long              6  fast
g  heavy             7  cheap
h  big               8  late

**6** Work with a partner. Take turns to say a word and your partner gives the opposite.

> expensive      cheap

**7** 2.16 Listen again to the conversation between Sophie and Henry and circle the correct answer.

a  Three hours is *okay / too long*.
b  Two hours is *too short / good*.
c  The Rex Hotel is *cheap / expensive*.
d  The Rialto Hotel is *expensive / cheap*.
e  The Regent Hotel is *expensive / great*.
f  Five o'clock is too *early / late*.

BUSINESS COMMUNICATION

## Do you like pizza?

**1** Label each photo with the words in the box.

cake   chicken   dessert   fish   pasta   pizza   salad   sandwiches

A _____   B _____   C _____   D _____

E _____   F _____   G _____   H _____

**2** What foods do you eat? Circle your answer.

a  Are you vegetarian?           Yes, I am. / No, I'm not.
b  Do you like salad?            Yes, I do. / No, I don't.
c  Do you like pizza?            Yes, I do. / No, I don't.
d  Do you eat fish?              Yes, I do. / No, I don't.
e  What desserts do you like?    Fruit / cheesecake / ice cream

**3** Work with a partner. Ask and answer the questions above.

**4** 2.17 Listen and tick (✓) the food Sophie and Dani talk about.

a cake ☐   c fish ☐   e pizza ☐   g sandwiches ☐
b chicken ☐   d pasta ☐   f salad ☐

**5** 2.17 Listen again and complete the sentences.

a  I need _____ food and drink for an event.
b  Do you have any _____ or _____?
c  _____ people are vegetarian.
d  We won't have _____ salad.
e  Let's have some _____.
f  _____ _____ _____ any dessert?

**6** Complete the sentences using *some* and *any*.

a  I think we need _____ dessert.
b  Do you have _____ salad?
c  I'm sorry, we don't have _____ sandwiches.
d  Do you have _____ cake?
e  I think we should have _____ pizza.
f  I don't have _____ chicken.

**7** Complete the table using *some* or *any*.

| | |
|---|---|
| positive (+) sentences | |
| negative (−) sentences | |
| questions (?) | |

### Natural language

When taking time to think in conversations, we often use short expressions:

*Hmm,   Well,   Okay,   Oh,   Erm,*

- *What date is good for the launch?*
- *Hmm, I'm not sure.*
- *Well, how about two months from now?*
- *Erm, yes, good idea.*
- *Okay, so now we need a venue. Any ideas?*
- *Oh, I don't know. What do you think?*

09 WHERE SHOULD I STAY?   65

**8** Complete the sentences about food for an event with your own ideas.

a Do you have any _____ or _____?
b I'm sorry, we don't have any _____.
c Do you want any _____?
d Okay, we won't have any _____.
e Let's have some _____ – that's a great idea.

**9** Practise ordering food for your event.

Speaker A: Look at page 84.    Speaker B: Look at page 85.

Use the phrases below in your conversation.

> Do you have any pizza?

> We don't have any pizza, but we do have some pasta. What about that?

> That sounds nice.

## Where should I go?

**1** Complete the words for each photo.

a city centre
b mus _ _ _ _
c art gal _ _ _ _ _
d sh _ _ _ ing ce _ _ re
e h _ _ _ _
f b _ _ ch

**2** 2.18 Listen to the conversations and tick (✓) the things they talk about.

|  | Conversation 1 | Conversation 2 |
| --- | --- | --- |
| The city centre |  |  |
| Museums and galleries |  |  |
| Shopping |  |  |
| Hotels |  |  |
| Beaches |  |  |

**3** 2.18 Listen again and complete the sentences using the words in the box.

should I    you can see    you could    you should

a _____ visit the city centre.
b _____ lots of museums and galleries.
c What _____ see there?
d _____ go to the bazaar, in the old city centre.

**4** Complete the sentences with the words in brackets in the correct order.

a _____ to the Museum of Culture. (go should you)
b _____ find a good restaurant? (can I where)
c _____ do in the city? (I should what)

---

**Writing tips**

Remember to use the correct preposition for time and place expressions.

*The event starts at 6 pm.* (use *at* for exact times)

*It's on Tuesday 23rd June.* (use *on* for days)

*Should we have our launch event in October?* (use *in* for longer time expressions including months and years)

*It's at the Hotel Royale/ in London.* (use *in* for most places)

## BUSINESS COMMUNICATION

**QUESTION TIME**
Write the missing words to complete the questions.
_____ should I do?
_____ should I stay?

**5** Write the sentences in the box next to the correct function.

| What should I do?   You could go to the beach.   Where can I eat?   You should visit the castle. |

**Asking for suggestions:** a _____
b _____

**Making suggestions:** c _____
d _____

**6** Write questions to ask for suggestions about what to do in another city.

a  should / stay
_Where should I stay?_

b  can / watch a football match
_____

c  should / visit
_____

d  can / buy clothes
_____

e  should / eat
_____

f  should / do
_____

**7** How can business visitors spend their free time in your city? Where can they stay? Write three or four suggestions for visitors.

You could _go to the castle in the city centre_.
You can go to _____.
You could go to _____.
You should visit _____.
How about visiting _____?

**8** Work with a partner. You are visiting their company. Prepare questions to ask about what to do, where to stay, etc.

Where do you work?

I work in Osaka.

What can I do there?

You could go to the castle in the city centre.

**09 WHERE SHOULD I STAY?** 67

# 09 Where should I stay?

### Vocabulary

## Opposites, food and places

**1** Write the opposites of the words.
a expensive _____
b good _____
c long _____
d early _____
e easy _____
f old _____

**2** Write the dishes in the box in the correct category.

cake   chicken   green salad

a dessert _____
b vegetarian _____
c meat _____

**3** Unscramble the letters to form words for food.
a z a z i p _____
b s p t a a _____
c t r e s d s e _____
d w i d a n h s c _____
e k i h c e n c _____
f d l a s a _____

**4** 🎧 2.19 Listen and write the words.
a _beach_
b _____
c _____
d _____
e _____
f _____
g _____
h _____

### Grammar

## Making suggestions and *some* and *any*

**1** Match the beginnings (a–e) to the endings (1–5) to make questions.

a Do           1 can I find an Indian restaurant?
b What         2 have some pizza.
c Let's        3 you like salad?
d Do           4 should I do in Paris?
e Where        5 you have any sandwiches?

**2** Which questions in 1 are used to ask for suggestions?

**3** Unscramble the words to make sentences.
a please / I'd / chicken, / some / like
_____
b do / salad / any / you / have?
_____
c should / you / stadium / visit / the
_____

**4** Circle the correct answer.
a I'd like *some / any* salad, please.
b Do you have *some / any* dessert?
c I'm sorry – there isn't *some / any* chicken.
d We have salad, and we also have *some / any* cheese.

### Pronunciation

## Stress to express likes and dislikes

**1** 🎧 2.20 Listen and repeat the sentences.
a I like salad.
b I don't like chicken.
c I like pizza, but I don't like sandwiches.

**2** 🎧 2.20 Listen again and underline the stressed words and syllables in 1.

### Using language

Tick (✓) the correct column for each sentence.

| | Asking | Suggesting | Agreeing |
|---|---|---|---|
| Do you have any pizza? | ✓ | | |
| Where should I stay? | | | |
| How about an expensive hotel? | | | |
| Yes, you're right. | | | |
| You should visit the old town. | | | |
| That's a good idea. | | | |
| What should I see in the city? | | | |

## LANGUAGE LINKS

**Phrase bank: Asking for suggestions**

a   Which one of the following questions is *not* asking for a suggestion?
    *What should I do there?*
    *Do you have any food?*
    *Where should I stay?*
    *Where should I eat?*

b   Which one of the following is *not* making a suggestion?
    *You should visit the river.*
    *How about visiting the old city?*
    *Do you like visiting museums?*
    *You can find a lot of restaurants in the city centre.*

### Writing

**Emailing a business visitor**

Complete the email to a business visitor from another city or country.

Dear _____,

It's great that you're visiting _____ next week! After our meeting, you can go and see a lot of places. You could _____ or you could _____. If you have time, you _____. You can find lots of _____ here, of course, and _____, too.

Best wishes,

_____

### Reviewing objectives

Tick (✓) the statements which are true for you.

I can plan food for a business event. ☐
I can ask for local information. ☐
I can give tips to business visitors. ☐

# My notes from Unit 09

# 10 Is cash okay?

> By fighting you never get enough, but by giving you get more than you expected.
>
> Dale Carnegie, communications expert

**Circle the correct option.**
Dale Carnegie thinks giving has *surprising* / *unsurprising* results.

### Learning objectives: Unit 10
**Business communication skills** Negotiating; Roleplay: Negotiating a deal
**Reading** Email about a negotiation; Contract
**Listening** Negotiations about delivery, price and discounts
**Vocabulary** Contract language
**Grammar** Talking about the future
**Phrase bank** Requesting, refusing and accepting
**In Company interviews** Units 9–10

## Can we talk about price?

**1** Read the email and tick (✓) the correct summary.

a Kathy wants to talk about the size of office chairs available. ☐
b Kathy wants to talk about the price and delivery times of office chairs. ☐
c Kathy wants to talk about the price and delivery times of office desks. ☐

---

**Chair Purchase**

To: John Kelly
From: Kathy Johnson

Hi John,

We'd like to buy some new office furniture. Can we meet next week to talk about the different options?

We want to buy 30 new chairs and we'd like to discuss prices and delivery times. Can we also talk about discounts and how to pay? We want to pay in cash but we could pay by bank transfer.

Thank you and I look forward to hearing from you.

Kind regards,
Kathy Johnson

Head of Purchasing
Harding's Ltd
Email: kathy.johnson@Hardings.com
Tel: 0044 207 635 8779

---

**2** Label each photo with words in the box.

bank transfer    cash    discount

a _____    b _____    c _____

**3** 🔊 2.21 Listen to John and Kathy discussing price and tick (✓) the correct summary.

a John and Kathy don't agree on anything. ☐
b John and Kathy agree on some things and disagree on some things. ☐
c John and Kathy agree on everything. ☐

70  10 IS CASH OKAY?

**Writing tips**

The most common ways to start an email are:
a Dear Mr Smith ___
b Dear John ___
c Hi John ___

Write *F* next to the formal ending, *N* next to the neutral ending and *I* next to the informal ending.

**4** 2.21 Listen again and decide if the sentences are true (*T*) or false (*F*).

a Kathy wants a 15% discount.    T / F
b John offers a 7% discount.    T / F
c Kathy wants to pay in 120 days.    T / F
d John asks Kathy to pay in 90 days.    T / F
e Kathy wants to pay by bank transfer.    T / F
f John wants to be paid in cash.    T / F

**5** 2.21 Listen again and complete the conversation with the words in the box.

| afraid | could | fine | like | okay | price | take | that's |

**Kathy:** Okay, that's agreed. Can we talk about (a) _____ now?
**John:** Sure, what do you want to talk about?
**Kathy:** Well, we'd (b) _____ a 10% discount.
**John:** Sorry, but (c) _____ difficult. We only give a 5% discount.
**Kathy:** That's (d) _____, we'll take 5%. (e) _____ we pay in 120 days?
**John:** I'm (f) _____ that's too long for us. What about 90 days?
**Kathy:** Okay, we'll (g) _____ 90 days. Is bank transfer okay?
**John:** That's (h) _____.
**Kathy:** Great. So, we'll pay in 90 days, by bank transfer, with a 5% discount, right?
**John:** That's right.

**6** Put the phrases below under the correct headings in the table.

a we'd like …
b sorry, but …
c … is a bit difficult
d could we …?
e that's fine
f okay, we'll take …
g is … okay?
h that's okay
i I'm afraid …

| Asking for something | Saying no politely | Accepting an offer |
|---|---|---|
| we'd like … | | |

**7** Complete the negotiation with the words in the box.

| a bit difficult | could | afraid | fine | like | okay | sorry | take | that's |

**A**

1 We'd _____ a 15% discount

**B**

2 I'm _____ we can only offer a 10% discount.

3 Okay, we'll _____ 10%. Can we pay by bank transfer?

4 _____, but we need to receive cash.

5 That's _____. We'll pay in cash. _____ we get delivery next week?

6 Sorry, that's _____. Is it _____ to deliver in two weeks?

7 Yes, _____ okay.

**8** Work with a partner and practise the negotiation in 7.

## Final details

**1** 🎧 **2.22** Listen to John and Kathy finalizing the contract. When will the delivery be? Circle the correct answers.

a Tuesday / Thursday
b 9th / 19th
c March / May

**2** 🎧 **2.22** Listen again and circle the correct answers for each of the sentences from the discussion.

a We'll use Tailor's.
*happen in the future / not happen in the future*
b Sorry but we won't pay all the delivery costs.
*happen in the future / not happen in the future*
c We'll pay fifty per cent each.
*happen in the future / not happen in the future*
d I'll phone you to confirm.
*happen in the future / not happen in the future*

**3** Read the contract and complete the sentences below using *will* or *won't*.

### CONTRACT

| | |
|---|---|
| **Parties:** | **Payment method:** |
| Kelly & Sons AND Harding's | Bank transfer |
| **Deliverables:** | **Delivery date:** |
| 30 office chairs | Monday 25th November |
| **Unit price:** | **Delivery company:** |
| £142.50 (£150 -5% discount) | Tailor's |
| **Payment period:** | **Payment of delivery costs:** |
| 90 days | 50% Kelly & Sons/50% Harding's |

a Kelly & Sons _will_ deliver 30 chairs.
b Harding's _____ get a 10% discount.
c Harding's _____ pay in 90 days.
d Harding's _____ pay in cash.
e The delivery _____ be on 25th November.
f Kelly & Sons _____ pay all the delivery costs

### ❓ QUESTION TIME

We can make questions about the future using *will*:
Kelly & Sons will deliver 30 chairs. *Will* Kelly & Sons ~~will~~ deliver 30 chairs?

**4** Rewrite the sentences in question form.

a Kelly & Sons will deliver the chairs.   _Will Kelly & Sons deliver the chairs?_
b Harding's will get a 15% discount.   _____
c The delivery will be on 25th November.   _____
d Tailor's will deliver the chairs.   _____
e Harding's will pay all the delivery costs.   _____
f Kelly & Sons will pay 50% of the delivery costs.   _____

**BUSINESS COMMUNICATION**

**5** Complete the table with *will* or *won't*.

| Positive | Negative | Question |
|---|---|---|
| I | I | I …? |
| You | You | you …? |
| He/She/It _____ | He/She/It _____ | _____ he/she/it …? |
| We | We | we …? |
| They | They | they …? |

**6** Work with a partner. Ask the questions in 4 and answer using the information in the contract in 3.

> Will Harding's get a 15% discount?

> No, they won't.

## Negotiating a deal

**1** Complete the negotiation using the words in the box.

afraid   but   can x2   deliver   difficult   like   okay   will

**A**                                                                                                **B**

1  When _____ you deliver the product?

2  We will _____ on Tuesday.

3  I'm _____ that's too late. _____ you deliver on Monday morning?

4  Sorry, _____ that's difficult. _____ Monday afternoon be okay?

5  That's fine. We'd _____ a 10% discount.

6  I'm afraid that's _____, but I'll check to see if it's possible.

7  _____, thanks. Will you phone me about the discount?

8  Yes, I'll phone you later.

### 💬 Natural language

When people ask a question with *will*, we can answer in different ways:

- 💬 Will you give us a discount?
- 💬 Yes, we will give you a discount. / No, we won't give you a discount.
- 💬 Yes, we will./ No, we won't.

**2** Work with a partner.
Speaker A: Reorganize the words into one or two sentences.
Speaker B: Look at page 84.

a  we'd 10% discount a like       *We'd like a 10% discount.*
b  okay that's / will we take 5%
c  deliver can you Thursday morning on?
d  afraid I'm we need on delivery Thursday
e  can pay days 120 in we?
f  fine that's / will pay we 90 in days
   like we'd pay cash to in
g  will we pay bank by transfer

📹 **In Company interviews Units 9–10**

**3** Work with your partner and negotiate a deal. Use the sentences above and respond to the answers.

> We'd like a 10% discount.

> I'm afraid we can only give a 5% discount.

**10 IS CASH OKAY?   73**

# 10 Is cash okay?

## Vocabulary

### Contract language

Complete the contract with the words in the box.

cost   date   deliverables   parties   payment   price

### CONTRACT

(a) _____: Watson's AND Office Supplies Ltd

(b) _____: 10 office desks

Unit (c) _____: £90

(d) _____ period: 120 days

Payment method: Cash

Delivery (e) _____: Thursday 18th July

Payment of delivery (f) _____: 50% Watson's/ 50% Office Supplies Ltd

## Grammar

### Talking about the future

**1** Write sentences about the future using *will/won't* and the information to help you.

a  I / get a new job (✓)    _I will get a new job._
b  we / get the contract (✗)  _____
c  we / make a profit (✓)    _____
d  I / get a pay rise (✗)     _____
e  we / hire new staff (✗)   _____
f  we / win the negotiation (✓)  _____

**2** Rewrite the sentences in 1 as questions about the future. Change all the sentences to questions with *will*.

a  _Will you get a new job?_
b  _____
c  _____
d  _____
e  _____
f  _____

### Using language

**1** Match the sentence beginnings (a–f) with the endings (1–6).

a  I'm afraid            1  a bit difficult.
b  Could we have         2  fine.
c  Sorry, but that's     3  we can't do that.
d  That's                4  pay in 90 days?
e  Is it okay to         5  give discounts.
f  Sorry, but we don't   6  a discount?

**2** Match these sentences to the sentences in 1.

1  I want a discount.           _b_
2  We can't do that.            ____
3  Good.                        ____
4  I'm afraid that isn't easy.  ____
5  Can we pay in 90 days?       ____
6  We don't give discounts.     ____

### Phrase bank: Requesting, refusing and accepting

**1** Draw arrows between the columns to make a short conversation.

| A | B | A |
|---|---|---|
| Could we pay in 90 days? | I'm afraid we need a bank transfer. | That's fine. We will pay by bank transfer. |
| We'd like a 15% discount. | 90 days is a bit difficult. | That's okay. We will pay in 60 days. |
| Is cash okay? | Sorry, but we only give 12% discounts. | Okay, we'll take 12%. |

**2** Complete the table with examples from 1 of people making, refusing and accepting requests.

| Making requests | *Could we pay in 90 days?* |
|---|---|
| Refusing requests | |
| Accepting requests | |

# LANGUAGE LINKS

## Pronunciation

### Connected speech

**1** 🎧 **2.23** Listen to the sentences and mark the linked sounds (where one word is joined to the next).

a  Could we pay in 90 days?
b  90 days is a bit difficult.
c  That's okay.
d  I'm afraid we need a bank transfer.
e  Is cash okay?

**2** 🎧 **2.23** Listen again and repeat the sentences.

## Writing

### Emailing contract information

Using the information in the contract, complete the email opposite.

### CONTRACT

| | |
|---|---|
| **Product:** | office desks (x27) |
| **Delivery date:** | Monday 27th November |
| **Discount:** | 20% |
| **Payment period:** | 30 days |
| **Payment method:** | bank transfer |

---

**Final Contract**

To: Paula Smith
From: John Kelly
Subject: Final contract
Attached: 📄 harding's_contract

Hi Paula,

We finished the negotiation with Harding's yesterday. Please check you are happy with the details below, and sign the attached.

We will deliver 27 (a) _____ on (b) _____.

We will give them a (c) _____ discount and they will pay in (d) _____.

They will pay by (e) _____.

Thanks,
John

### Reviewing objectives

Tick (✓) the statements which are true for you.

| | |
|---|---|
| I can talk about the future. | ☐ |
| I can ask questions about the future. | ☐ |
| I can negotiate costs and delivery terms. | ☐ |
| I can accept and refuse offers and requests. | ☐ |

---

## My notes from Unit 10

## SURVIVAL SCENARIO E

**Learning objectives: Workplace Scenario E**

**Business communication skills**
Describing food; Talking about food from different countries; Fluency: Describing a dish from your country or region
**Reading** Menu of a British restaurant
**In Company in action**
E1: How about a British restaurant?;
E2: Tell us about Spanish food

In Company in action

---

### THE GOLDEN GOOSE

#### MENU

##### STARTERS

Soup of the day
Please see the (1) _____.

Mackerel paté
With a choice of
(2) _____ or crackers.

##### MAIN COURSES

Fish pie
Cod and vegetables, with
(3) _____ potato.

Beef Wellington
Steak, mushrooms and paté in
(4) _____.

---

# What's Eton mess?

**1** Choose at least one adjective from the box for each dish.

| fresh | healthy | heavy | salty | spicy | sweet | sour |

a _____  c _____  e _____

b _____  d _____  f _____

**2** Complete the menu on the left with words from the box.

| board | bread | mashed | pastry |

**3** Tomorrow is Antonio's last day in the UK. The BetterDrinks team plan a meal to say goodbye to him. Watch video E1. <u>Underline</u> the dishes on the menu in 2 which they talk about.

**4** Read the sentences and (circle) the correct answer. Watch video E1 again to check your answers.

a Caroline has *a few / no* ideas for restaurants.
b Karl thinks Antonio *wants / doesn't want* to eat Spanish food in the UK.
c Caroline says beef Wellington is *heavy / healthy*.
d Beef Wellington has got *mushrooms / chocolate* in it.

**5** Match the sentence beginnings (a–d) with the endings (1–4).

a Pasta is a kind of                          1 Korean food.
b You can get sushi at that                   2 Spanish restaurant.
c Kimchi is my favourite kind of              3 Italian food.
d I always choose paella when I go to a       4 Japanese restaurant.

## SURVIVAL SCENARIO

**6** Match the questions (a–d) to the answers (1–4).

a  What's pastry?
b  What's in paella?
c  What is sushi made with?
d  What has borscht got in it?

1  It's made with rice and raw fish.
2  There's rice, and sometimes there's seafood, or sometimes there's chicken or vegetables.
3  The main ingredient is beetroot, and it often has potatoes or cabbage.
4  It's used to make pies and it's made with flour and eggs.

**7** Here is a conversation between two people in a restaurant.

a  Work with a partner and practise reading the conversation.

**A**

1  What do you want to eat?

3  What's in <u>paella</u>?

5  Sounds good. Where's it from?

**B**

2  I want to eat <u>paella</u>.

4  <u>There's rice, and sometimes there's seafood, or sometimes there's chicken or vegetables.</u>

6  It's <u>Spanish</u>.

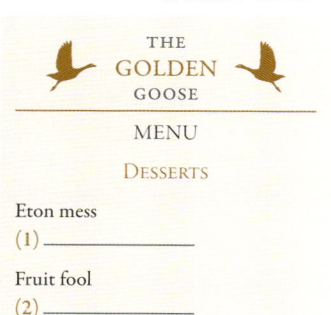

b  Now change roles, and replace the underlined words with words from 5 and 6.

**8** The BetterDrinks team take Antonio for a British meal at the The Golden Goose. Watch video E2 and match the desserts in the menu to the descriptions below.

a  Summer fruits, cream and sugar.
b  Cream, meringue and strawberries.

**In Company in action**

### THE GOLDEN GOOSE
#### MENU
#### DESSERTS

Eton mess
(1) _____

Fruit fool
(2) _____

**9** Write one word to complete each of the sentences. Watch video E2 again to check your answers.

a  Now, what do you want to eat for _____?
b  I think that Eton mess _____ got strawberries and meringue in it.
c  Oh, it's delicious. It's _____ with egg and sugar. I think it's French.
d  So, there are many types of _____. Meat, fish, or vegetables.
e  It's a little spicy. It's quite _____ but very good.

**Useful language:**
It's light/heavy/spicy …
It's made with …
It's a dessert/main course/starter.
It's got …

**10** Work with a partner. Practise the dialogues.

a  Think about a typical dish from your country or region. Prepare to describe it to your partner. Make notes in the space below.

_____
_____
_____
_____

b  Describe the dish to your partner.

Evaluate your performance using the **Reviewing objectives** box on page 84.

# Irregular verb list

| Verb | Past Simple | Past Participle |
|---|---|---|
| arise | arose | arisen |
| be | was, were | been |
| bear | bore | borne |
| beat | beat | beaten |
| become | became | become |
| begin | began | begun |
| bend | bent | bent |
| bet | bet | bet |
| bid | bid | bid |
| bind | bound | bound |
| bite | bit | bitten/bit |
| bleed | bled | bled |
| blow | blew | blown |
| break | broke | broken |
| breed | bred | bred |
| bring | brought | brought |
| broadcast | broadcast | broadcast |
| build | built | built |
| burn | burnt/burned | burnt/burned |
| burst | burst | burst |
| buy | bought | bought |
| catch | caught | caught |
| choose | chose | chosen |
| come | came | come |
| cost | cost | cost |
| creep | crept | crept |
| cut | cut | cut |
| deal | dealt | dealt |
| dig | dug | dug |
| do | did | done |
| draw | drew | drawn |
| dream | dreamt/dreamed | dreamt/dreamed |
| drink | drank | drunk |
| drive | drove | driven |
| eat | ate | eaten |
| fall | fell | fallen |
| feed | fed | fed |
| feel | felt | felt |
| fight | fought | fought |
| find | found | found |
| flee | fled | fled |
| fly | flew | flown |
| forbid | forbade | forbidden |
| forecast | forecast | forecast |
| forget | forgot | forgotten |
| forgive | forgave | forgiven |
| freeze | froze | frozen |
| get | got | got/gotten |
| give | gave | given |
| go | went | gone |
| grind | ground | ground |
| grow | grew | grown |
| hang | hung | hung |
| have | had | had |
| hear | heard | heard |
| hide | hid | hidden |
| hit | hit | hit |
| hold | held | held |
| hurt | hurt | hurt |
| keep | kept | kept |
| kneel | knelt/kneeled | knelt/kneeled |
| know | knew | known |
| lay | laid | laid |
| lead | led | led |
| lean | leant/leaned | leant/leaned |
| leap | leapt/leaped | leapt/leaped |
| learn | learnt/learned | learnt/learned |
| leave | left | left |
| lend | lent | lent |
| let | let | let |
| lie | lay | lain |
| light | lit/lighted | lit/lighted |
| lose | lost | lost |
| make | made | made |
| mean | meant | meant |
| meet | met | met |
| mislead | misled | misled |
| misspell | misspelt/misspelled | misspelt/misspelled |
| misunderstand | misunderstood | misunderstood |
| overcome | overcame | overcome |

# IRREGULAR VERB LIST

| Verb | Past Simple | Past Participle |
|---|---|---|
| overhear | overheard | overheard |
| overspend | overspent | overspent |
| overtake | overtook | overtaken |
| pay | paid | paid |
| prove | proved | proven/proved |
| put | put | put |
| quit | quit | quit |
| read | read | read |
| ride | rode | ridden |
| ring | rang | rung |
| rise | rose | risen |
| run | ran | run |
| say | said | said |
| see | saw | seen |
| seek | sought | sought |
| sell | sold | sold |
| send | sent | sent |
| set | set | set |
| sew | sewed | sewn |
| shake | shook | shaken |
| shine | shone | shone |
| shoot | shot | shot |
| show | showed | shown |
| shrink | shrank | shrunk |
| shut | shut | shut |
| sing | sang | sung |
| sit | sat | sat |
| sleep | slept | slept |
| slide | slid | slid |
| smell | smelt/smelled | smelt/smelled |
| speak | spoke | spoken |
| speed | sped/speeded | sped/speeded |
| spell | spelt/spelled | spelt/spelled |
| spend | spent | spent |
| spill | spilt/spilled | spilt/spilled |
| spin | spun | spun |
| spit | spat | spat |
| split | split | split |
| spoil | spoilt/spoiled | spoilt/spoiled |
| spread | spread | spread |

| Verb | Past Simple | Past Participle |
|---|---|---|
| spring | sprang | sprung |
| stand | stood | stood |
| steal | stole | stolen |
| stick | stuck | stuck |
| sting | stung | stung |
| strike | struck | struck |
| swear | swore | sworn |
| sweep | swept | swept |
| swim | swam | swum |
| swing | swung | swung |
| take | took | taken |
| teach | taught | taught |
| tear | tore | torn |
| tell | told | told |
| think | thought | thought |
| throw | threw | thrown |
| understand | understood | understood |
| wake | woke | woken |
| wear | wore | worn |
| weep | wept | wept |
| win | won | won |
| wind | wound | wound |
| withdraw | withdrew | withdrawn |
| withhold | withheld | withheld |
| write | wrote | written |

Note: where two alternative forms are given, the second form is used in American English.

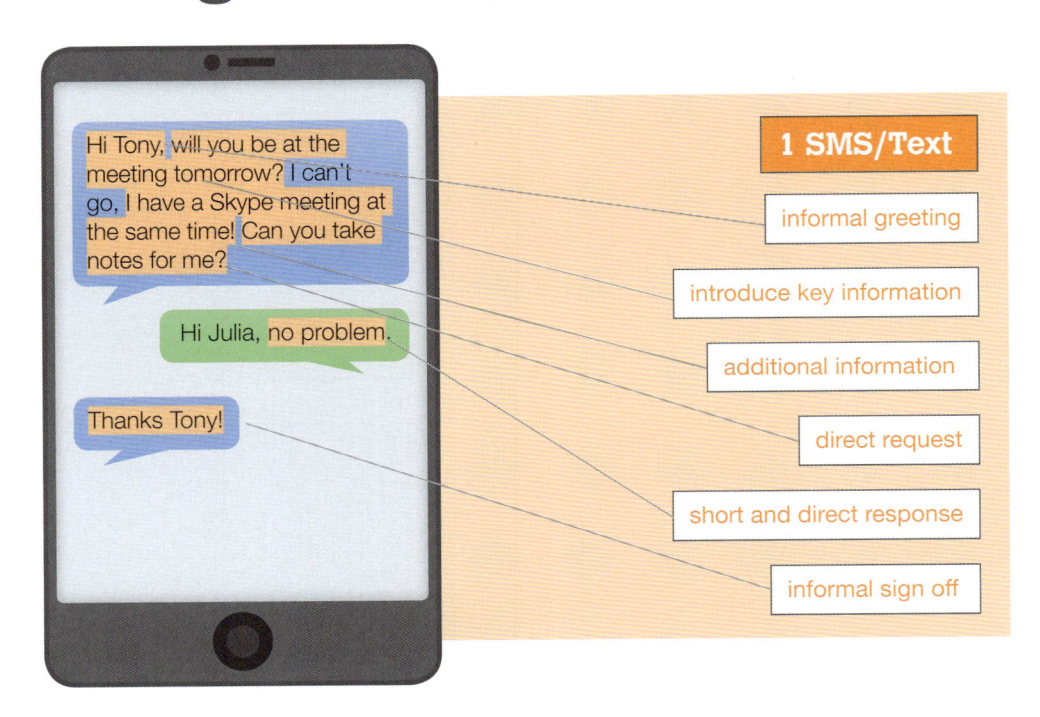

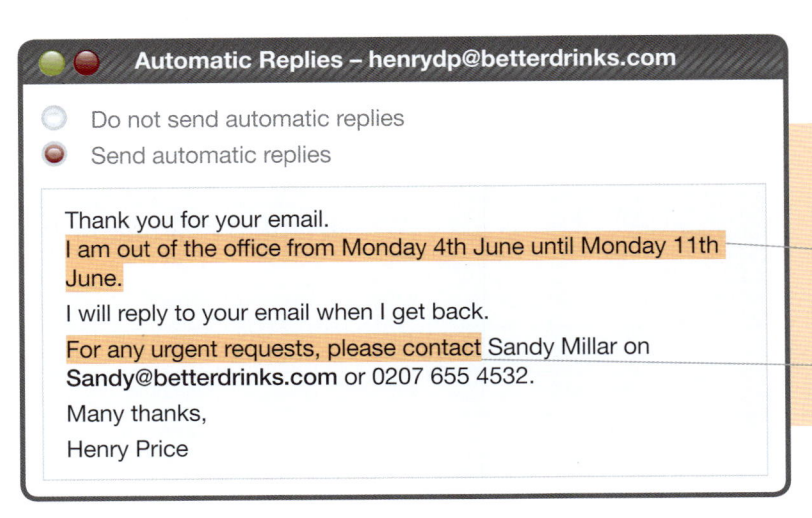

# Writing bank

## 1 SMS/Text

> Hi Tony, will you be at the meeting tomorrow? I can't go, I have a Skype meeting at the same time! Can you take notes for me?
>
> Hi Julia, no problem.
>
> Thanks Tony!

- informal greeting
- introduce key information
- additional information
- direct request
- short and direct response
- informal sign off

## 2 Out of office reply

**Automatic Replies – henrydp@betterdrinks.com**

○ Do not send automatic replies
● Send automatic replies

Thank you for your email.
I am out of the office from Monday 4th June until Monday 11th June.
I will reply to your email when I get back.
For any urgent requests, please contact Sandy Millar on Sandy@betterdrinks.com or 0207 655 4532.
Many thanks,
Henry Price

- key information: dates of absence and return
- give colleague's contact details

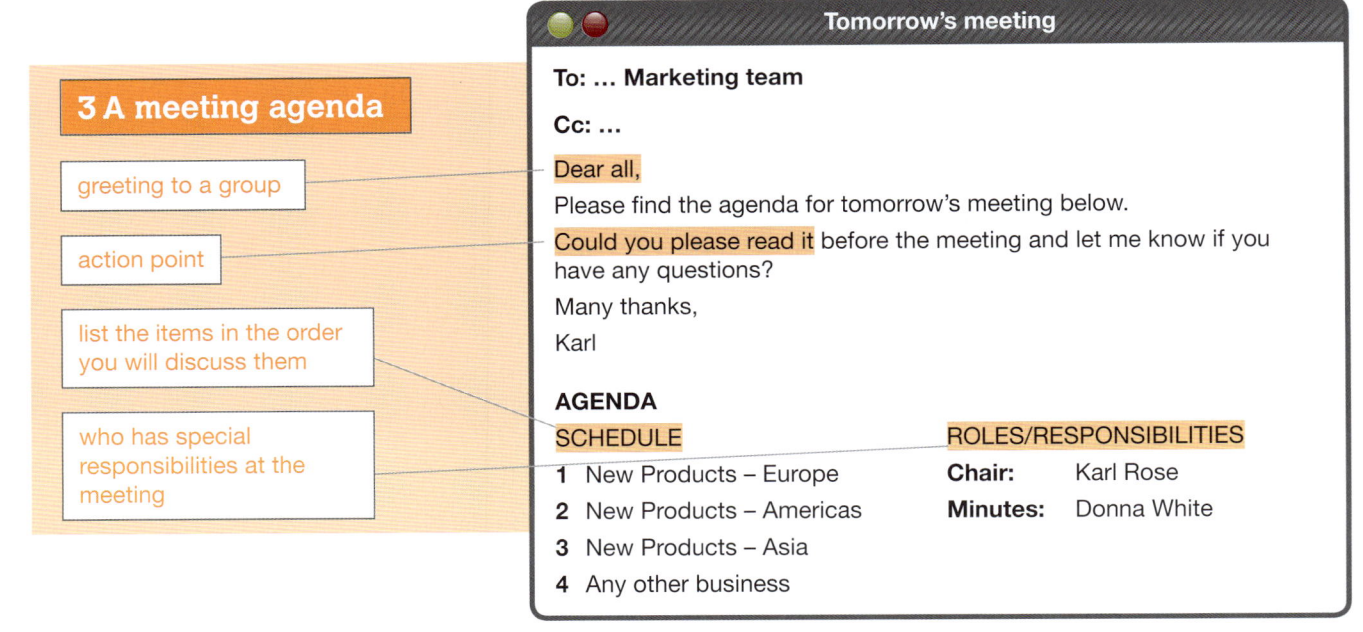

## 3 A meeting agenda

- greeting to a group
- action point
- list the items in the order you will discuss them
- who has special responsibilities at the meeting

**Tomorrow's meeting**

**To:** … Marketing team
**Cc:** …

Dear all,
Please find the agenda for tomorrow's meeting below.
Could you please read it before the meeting and let me know if you have any questions?
Many thanks,
Karl

**AGENDA**

| SCHEDULE | ROLES/RESPONSIBILITIES | |
|---|---|---|
| 1 New Products – Europe | Chair: | Karl Rose |
| 2 New Products – Americas | Minutes: | Donna White |
| 3 New Products – Asia | | |
| 4 Any other business | | |

WRITING BANK

# WRITING BANK

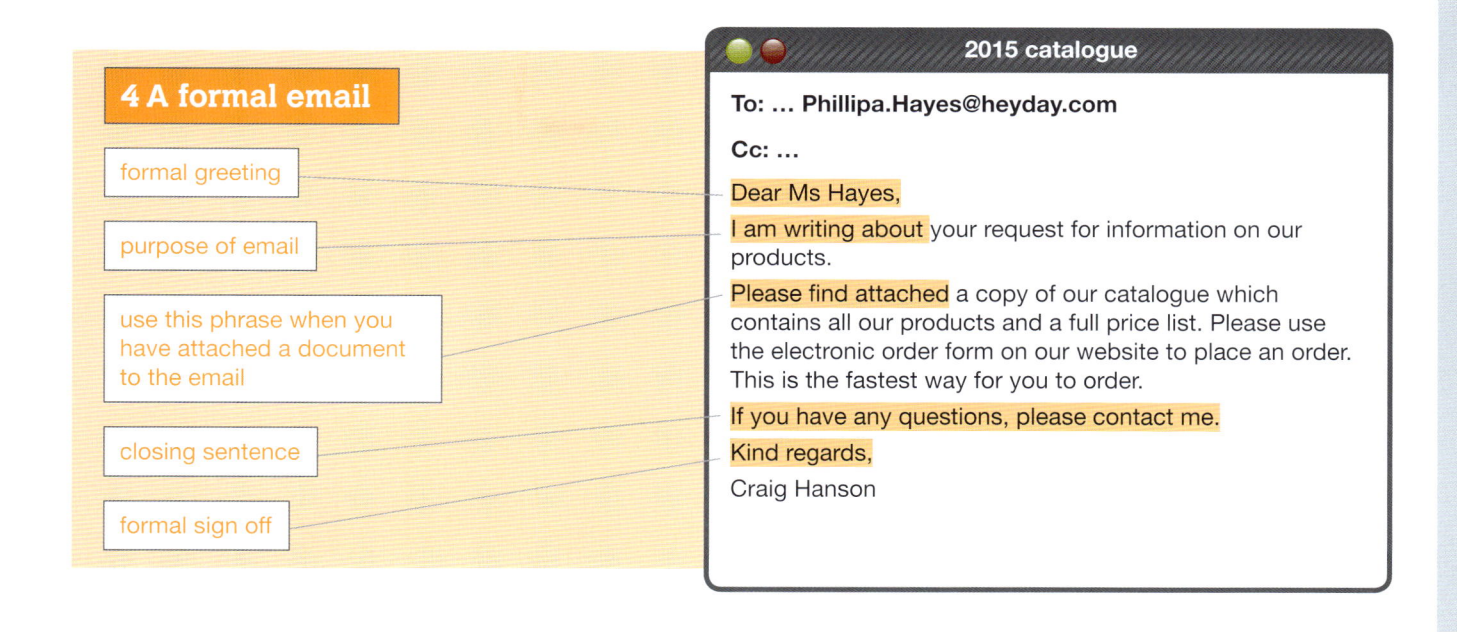

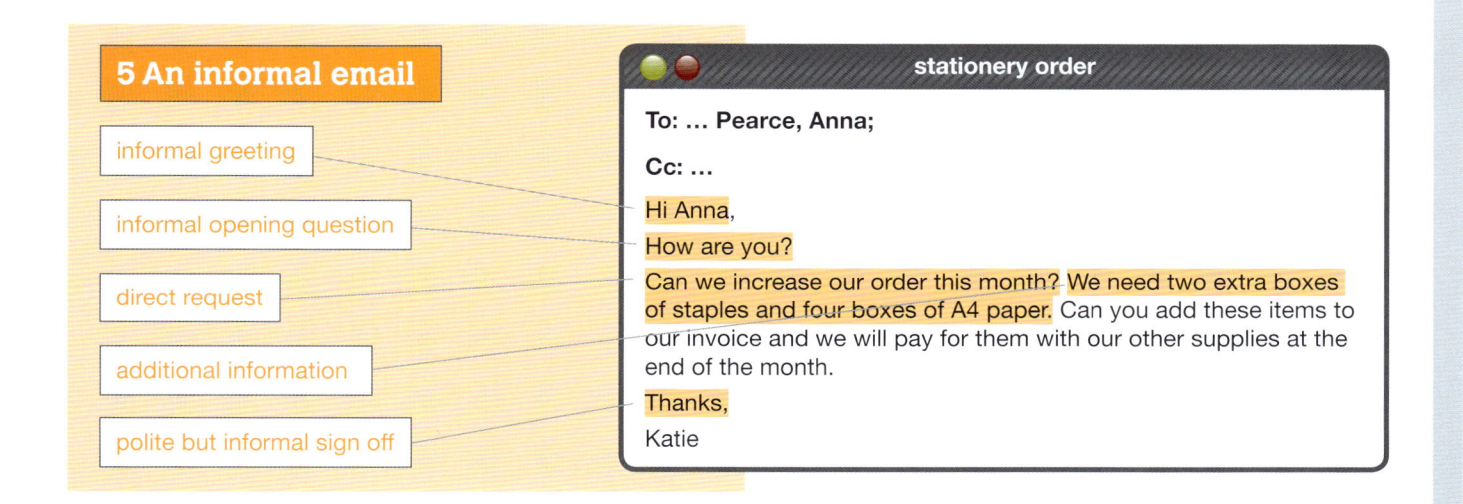

## 4 A formal email

- formal greeting
- purpose of email
- use this phrase when you have attached a document to the email
- closing sentence
- formal sign off

**2015 catalogue**

To: … Phillipa.Hayes@heyday.com
Cc: …

Dear Ms Hayes,

I am writing about your request for information on our products.

Please find attached a copy of our catalogue which contains all our products and a full price list. Please use the electronic order form on our website to place an order. This is the fastest way for you to order.

If you have any questions, please contact me.

Kind regards,

Craig Hanson

## 5 An informal email

- informal greeting
- informal opening question
- direct request
- additional information
- polite but informal sign off

**stationery order**

To: … Pearce, Anna;
Cc: …

Hi Anna,

How are you?

Can we increase our order this month? We need two extra boxes of staples and four boxes of A4 paper. Can you add these items to our invoice and we will pay for them with our other supplies at the end of the month.

Thanks,

Katie

## 6 Minutes

- who came to the meeting
- key point
- more detail about key point
- who will do the action
- deadline

| | |
|---|---|
| **Date:** | 28th September |
| **Time:** | 0900–1345 |
| **Chair:** | Maria Ripoli |
| **Attendees:** | Maria Ripoli, Sarah Millar, Dave Watson, Enrico Falconio |

| | | | |
|---|---|---|---|
| Item 1: | New head of Finance | Sarah Millar will become the new head of finance next week. | **Action:** None |
| Item 2: | Future business trips | Dave Watson talked about his sales trip to the USA and listed key customers. | **Action:** Dave Watson to report on progress after trip. |
| Item 3: | Annual General Meeting | The AGM will be on 4th December. The company will invite all shareholders. Shareholders will receive invitations by letter and email next week. | **Action:** Enrico Falconio will send emails and letters to all shareholders by Friday. |

WRITING BANK  81

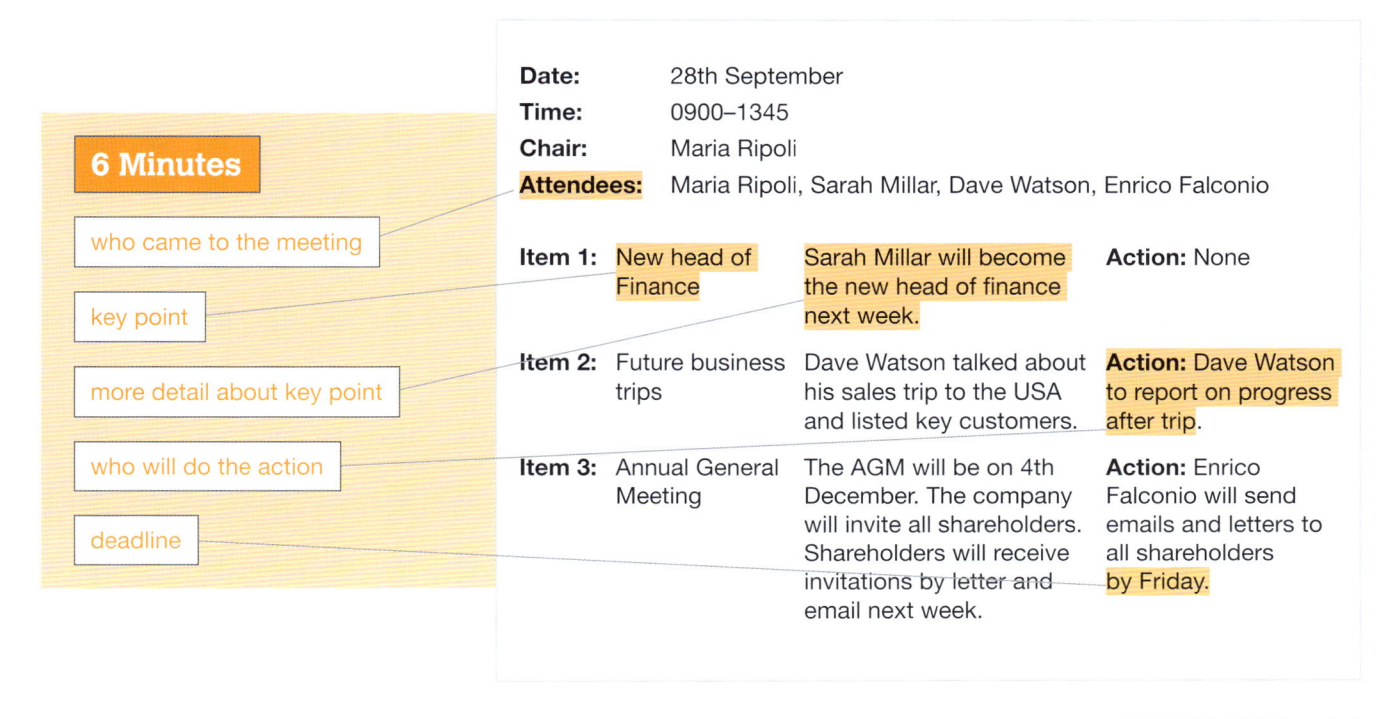

# Additional material

## 01 Sara, this is Ed
### Letters and names (p9, ex7)

**Speaker A:** Imagine you are registering at a networking event. Spell these names to your partner.

Mark Smith

Lisa Matheson

(your name)

Now write the names your partner spells.

_____   _____   _____

## 04 Can I Help You?
### Days, months and dates (p31, ex13)

**Speaker A:** You want to arrange a meeting with Speaker B. Look at your calendar. When can you meet them? Telephone Speaker B and try to arrange a meeting.

|           | Monday                         | Tuesday              | Wednesday       | Thursday              | Friday                         |
|-----------|--------------------------------|----------------------|-----------------|-----------------------|--------------------------------|
| Morning   | a meeting with clients         | a team meeting       | a team meeting  | a meeting with clients |                                |
| Afternoon | a lunch meeting with my manager| a conference call    |                 | a shopping trip       | a lunch meeting with team      |
| Evening   | football practice              | tickets for a show   | sales training  | football practice     | a dinner meeting with clients  |

> Can we meet on Tuesday morning?

> Sorry, I have a team meeting on Tuesday morning.

## Scenario B, It's very close
### (p35, ex10)

**Speaker B:** Use the map to answer your partner's questions.

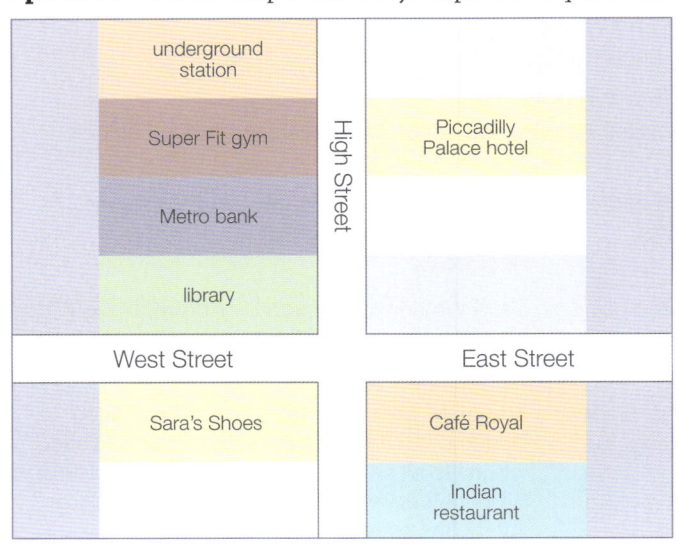

Now ask your partner where these places are and write them in the correct space on your map:

department store    post office    Turkish restaurant

# 08 I'd like to talk about …
## Q&A (p59, ex10)
**Speaker A**

**1** Use the graph to complete the sentences below.

**Investment by quarter**

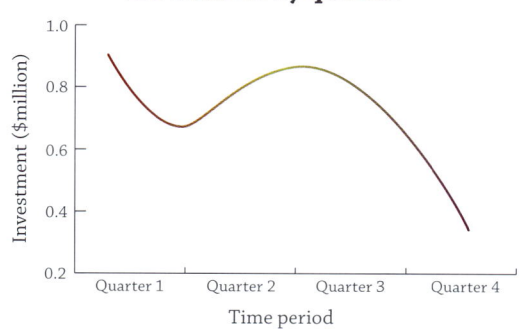

a   Sales _____ in quarter 1.
b   Sales _____ in quarter 2.
c   Sales _____ in quarter 3.
d   Sales _____ in quarter 4.

**2** Use your graph and the ideas below to create a short presentation. Use the graph to answer your partner's questions.

a   Today, I'd like to present the sales results.
b   First, I'll explain quarter 1. In quarter 1, sales …
c   Now, I'll outline …
d   Now, I'll …
e   Finally, I'll …
f   To recap, …

**3** Use the prompts to create questions for your partner's presentation.

a   investment / increase / quarter 1?
b   investment / go up / quarter 2?
c   investment / fall / quarter 3?
d   investment / grow / quarter 4?

**4** Take turns giving a short presentation and asking your questions from 3.

# 09 Where should I stay?
## The launch party (p64, ex3)

Complete the invitation with your ideas.

**INVITATION**

You are invited to the launch of our new _____ business: _____

At _____
On _____
From _____
Please reply to _____

## Scenario D, Click the icon
### (p63, ex11)

**Reviewing objectives**

Tick (✓) the statements which are true for you.

I can give instructions for a common office task. ☐
I can respond to instructions for common office tasks. ☐

## Scenario A, Enjoy your stay
### (p21, ex10)

**Speaker B**
**Conversation 1**
You are the receptionist.
Ask for the guest's name and their passport.
They have a reservation for three nights.
Their room number is 306 – on the third floor.
The restaurant is on the second floor. It opens at 19:00 and closes at 23:30.

**Conversation 2**
You are the guest.
You have a reservation for four nights.
Check in to the hotel.
You want to know about breakfast. Ask where it is and what time it starts.

## Scenario C, Don't mention it
(p49, ex11)

**Reviewing objectives**

Tick (✓) the statements which are true for you.

I can ask someone a favour. ☐

I can respond to a request for a favour. ☐

## 09 Where should I stay?
### Do you like pizza? (p66, ex9)

**Speaker A**

**Part 1**

Your event is tomorrow!

Your partner is a caterer.

You need three types of food for your event.

Ask your partner if they have the following:

fish    pasta    pizza    sandwiches

Start the conversation:

*I need some food for an event tomorrow.*

Use the phrases on page 65 to help you.

Write the food you choose here:

_____  _____  _____

**Part 2**

You are a caterer.

Your partner is having an event tomorrow.

You only have the following food available:

chicken    pasta    sandwiches

Your partner will start the conversation. Respond with:

*What do you need?*

Use the phrases on page 66 to help you.

## 01 Sara, this is Ed
### Letters and names (p9, ex7)

**Speaker B:** Imagine you are registering at a networking event. Spell these names to your partner.

Beatrice Cole    Ben James    (your name)

Now write the names your partner spells.

_____

_____

_____

## 10 Is cash okay?
### Negotiating a deal (p73, ex2)

**Speaker B:** Reorganize the words into one or two sentences.

a   afraid I'm can we only a 5% give discount.
    *I'm afraid we can only give a 5% discount.*

b   fine that's / will we give a you 5% discount.
    _____

c   sorry no / can we deliver Friday on morning.
    _____

d   will we deliver okay Thursday on afternoon.
    _____

e   you can pay 90 in days?
    _____

f   difficult That's / you can pay bank by transfer?
    _____

g   agreed that's okay.
    _____

Listen to your partner's offers and respond using the sentences above.

> We'd like a 10% discount.

> I'm afraid we can only give a 5% discount.

## Scenario E, What's Eton mess?
(p77, ex11)

**Reviewing objectives**

Tick (✓) the statements which are true for you.

I can talk about food from different countries. ☐

I can describe a dish from my country. ☐

## 08 I'd like to talk about …
### Q&A (p59, ex10)
**Speaker B**

1 Use the graph to complete the sentences below.

**Investment by quarter**

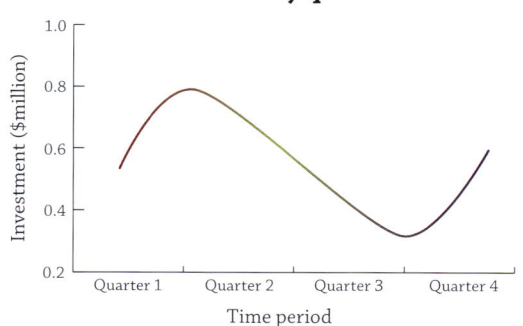

a Sales _____ in quarter 1.
b Sales _____ in quarter 2.
c Sales _____ in quarter 3.
d Sales _____ in quarter 4.

2 Use your graph and the ideas below to create a short presentation. Use the graph to answer your partner's questions.

a Today, I'd like to present investment rates in our company.
b First, I'll explain quarter 1. In quarter 1, profits …
c Now, I'll outline …
d Now, I'll …
e Finally I'll …
f To recap, …

3 Use the prompts to create questions for your partner's presentation.

a sales / go up / quarter 1?
b sales / get worse / quarter 2?
c sales / decrease / quarter 3?
d sales / rise / quarter 4?

4 Take turns giving a short presentation and asking your questions from 3.

## Scenario A, Enjoy your stay
### (p21, ex11)

**Reviewing objectives**

Tick (✓) the statements which are true for you.

I can check in to a hotel. ☐
I can ask questions about hotel facility opening times. ☐

## 09 Where should I stay?
### Do you like pizza? (p66, ex9)
**Speaker B**
**Part 1**

You are a caterer.
Your partner is having an event tomorrow.
You only have the following food available:

cake    salad    sandwiches

Your partner will start the conversation. Respond with:
*What do you need?*
Use the phrases on page 66 to help you.

**Part 2**

Your event is tomorrow!
Your partner is a caterer.
You need three types of food for your event.
Ask your partner if they have the following:

cake    fish    pizza    salad    sandwiches

Start the conversation:
*I need some food for an event tomorrow.*
Use the phrases on page 65 to help you.
Write the food you choose here:

_____    _____    _____

## Scenario B, It's very close
### (p35, ex11)

**Reviewing objectives**

Tick (✓) the statements which are true for you.

I can say where places in town are. ☐
I can say where places in an office are. ☐
I can ask where places in town are. ☐

## 04 Can I help you?

### Days, months and dates (p31, ex13)

**Speaker B:** Speaker A will telephone you to arrange a meeting. Look at your calendar. When can you meet them?

|           | Monday                  | Tuesday                   | Wednesday  | Thursday                      | Friday            |
|-----------|-------------------------|---------------------------|------------|-------------------------------|-------------------|
| Morning   | a conference call       |                           | a day off  | a team meeting                |                   |
| Afternoon | a meeting with clients  | a lunch meeting with clients | a day off  | a meeting with my manager     | a conference call |
| Evening   | tickets for the cinema  | a gym class               | a day off  | a dinner meeting with a client |                   |

Take the telephone call from Speaker A and try to arrange a meeting.

> Can we meet on Wednesday morning?

> Sorry, I have a day off on Wednesday.

---

## Scenario D, Click the icon
### (p63, ex10)
**Speaker A**

**1** Tell your partner how to send an email. Use the pictures to help you.

Useful language
Enter …          Type …
Click …          Choose …
Open …

**2** Listen to your partner's instructions and put the pictures in the correct order.

Useful language
I don't understand.       What was that?
Could you repeat that?    I see.

## Scenario B, It's very close
### (p35, ex10)

**Speaker A:** Ask your partner where these places are and write them in the correct space on your map:
Piccadilly Palace hotel
Indian restaurant
library

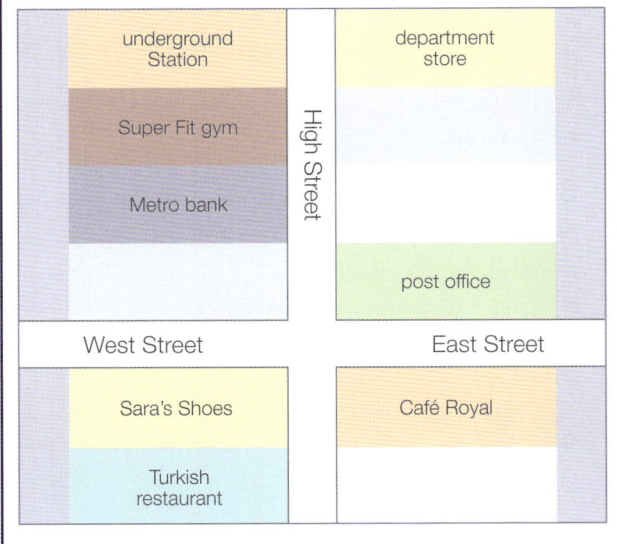

Now use the map to answer your partner's questions.

# Scenario C, Don't mention it
(p49, ex10)

**Speaker A**

**1** Ask your partner for a favour. Use the ideas in the box to help you.

| borrow a pen | start class late | use your computer |

Useful language

I need to …
Can I/you …
…is it okay?
The problem is …
Do you think I/you can …
Thank you for your help.

**2** Listen to your partner ask you a favour and respond.

Useful language

That's fine.
All right.
Sure. No problem.
Yes, I suppose I can do it.
I'm busy at the moment. Can you ask me later?
Don't mention it.

# Scenario A, Enjoy your stay
(p21, ex9)

**Conversation 1**

**A   Receptionist**                                           **Guest   B**

1  Good evening. Welcome to The Western Hotel.

                         2  Say you have a reservation
                         I have a reservation.

3  Can I take your name, please?

                         4  Say your name

5  Can you spell that for me, please?

                         6  Spell your name

7  Do you have your passport?

                         8  Give your passport

9  Your room number is five oh two.

**Conversation 2**

**A   Receptionist**                                           **Guest   B**

                         1  When's breakfast?

2  Say the times for breakfast
Breakfast is from …

                         3  Where is it?

4  Say where breakfast is

                         5  Is there a gym?

6  Tell the guest about the gym

7  Ask if they need more help

                         8  No, thanks.

## Scenario D, Click the icon
**(p63, ex10)**

**Speaker B**

**1** Listen to your partner's explanation and put the pictures in the correct order.

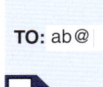

Useful language

I don't understand.     What was that?
Could you repeat that?  I see

**2** Tell your partner how to print a document using the pictures to help you.

Useful language

Choose ...      Type ...
Click ...       Collect ...
Open ...

## Scenario C, Don't mention it
**(p49, ex10)**

**Speaker B**

**1** Listen to your partner ask you a favour and respond.

Useful language

That's fine.
All right.
Sure. No problem.
Yes, I suppose I can do it.
I'm busy at the moment. Can you ask me later?
Don't mention it.

**2** Ask your partner for a favour. Use the ideas in the box to help you.

| borrow a pen | start class late | use your computer |

Useful language

I need to ...
Can I/you ...
...is it okay?
The problem is ...
Do you think I/you can ...
Thank you for your help.

## Scenario A, Enjoy your stay
**(p21, ex10)**

**Speaker A**

**Conversation 1**

You are the guest.
You have a reservation for three nights.
Check in to the hotel.
You want to have dinner in the restaurant. Ask where it is and what time it opens.

**Conversation 2**

You are the receptionist.
Ask for the guest's name and their passport.
They have a reservation for four nights.
Their room number is 404 – on the fourth floor.
Breakfast is in the restaurant. It starts at 07:30 and ends at 10:00.

ADDITIONAL MATERIAL

# Listening scripts

## 01 SARA, THIS IS ED

### 1.01

**Conversation 1**
A  Hello, what's your name?
B  Eva.
A  Nice to meet you. I'm Sara.
B  Nice to meet you.

**Conversation 2**
A  Hi, what's your name?
B  Juan. And you?
A  I'm Ed.
B  Good to meet you, Ed.

### 1.02

A  Hello, what's your name?
B  Eva.
A  Nice to meet you.

### 1.03

**Conversation 1**
A  Hello, I'm Ed.
B  Nice to meet you, Ed.
A  You too. And what's your name?
B  I'm Eva.
A  Great to meet you, Eve.
B  No, Eva.
A  Oh, sorry. Great to meet you, Eva.

**Conversation 2**
A  Hi, I'm Sara.
B  Nice to meet you, Sara. I'm Fatma.
A  Nice to meet you, Fatma.

**Conversation 3**
A  What's your name?
B  Juan.
A  Good to meet you. And what's your name?
B  I'm Stefan.
A  Great to meet you, Stefan.

### 1.04

A B C D E F G H I J K L M N O P Q R S T U V W X Y Z

### 1.05

A H J K
B C D E G P T V
F L M N S X Z
I Y
O
Q U W
R

### 1.06

1 USA    2 UK    3 EU    4 UN
5 WHO    6 CC    7 CEO   8 FAQ
9 PDF   10 HSBC 11 CFO
12 BBC

### 1.07

**Conversation 1**
A  Hello, I'm Juan. Juan Simons.
B  Hello, Juan. Welcome to our networking event. Can you spell your name please?
A  Yes, of course, J–U–A–N, Juan. And my surname is Simons, S–I–M–O–N–S.
B  Thank you. Now let me see, Simons, Simons…

**Conversation 2**
A  Good afternoon. What's your name?
B  I'm Sara. Sara Henley.
A  Thank you. Sara Hat… Ham… Ah, yes, H–E–N–L–E–Y. Is that correct?
B  Yes, that's right. Thank you.

**Conversation 3**
A  Hi, I'm Ed.
B  Hello, Ed. What's your surname?
A  It's Marcel. Ed Marcel.
B  Can you spell your surname, please?
A  Yes, it's M–A–R–C–E–L.
B  Thank you. Oh, sorry, *C* or *S*?
A  *C*.
B  Thank you.

### 1.08

**Conversation 1**
A  Hi, Sara.
B  Hello, Juan.
A  Sara, this is Carolina.
B  Good to meet you, Carolina.
C  You too. Nice to meet you, Sara.

**Conversation 2**
A  Hello, I'm George.
B  I'm Sara. Great to meet you, George.
A  You too. Oh, Sara, this is my colleague, Ed.
B  Great to meet you, Ed.
C  And you, Sara.

**Conversation 3**
A  Hi, George. George, meet Chris. Chris, this is George.
B  Hello, Chris. Nice to meet you.
C  You too, George.
A  Great. Chris is the executive…

### 1.09

**About us**
The Teambuilding Company offers you a great team-building experience. We can help you with all your team-building needs – from meeting people to building new teams for your company. Our team is ready to help you. Contact us now!

### 1.10

a  Is George your manager?
   George? No, he isn't.
b  Is your manager here?
   Yes, she is.
c  What's her name?
   Her name's Jane. Jane Goodwin.

### 1.11

A  Good evening. Can I take your name, please?
B  Verity Sambell.
A  Verity Sambell. Welcome to our event. And can I take your name, please?
C  Sure. I'm Gary Swales.
A  Thank you, Mr Swales. Good evening, can I take your name, please?
D  I'm Jasmine. Jasmine Soutern.
A  Thank you very much. Hello…

### 1.12

a  Hi, I'm David. Good to meet you.
b  My manager is Juan. He's great.
c  Can you spell your surname, please?
   Certainly. It's G–A–L–E.
d  Hello, Sarah. Is Jeremy your manager?
e  Are you Ahmed?
   No, I'm Mohammed.
f  Kate, this is Gunter. Gunter, meet Kate.

### 1.13

a  Can you spell that, please?
   Sure, it's K–I–E–R–A–N.
b  Hello. I'm David Cruze.
   That's C–R–U–Z–E.
c  And your surname, please.
   It's Rosebush. R–O–S–E–B–U–S–H.
d  My company is Springleigh. It's a design company. That's S–P–R–I–N–G–L–E–I–G–H. All one word.

## 02 I START WORK AT 8 AM

### 1.14

| One | Two | Three | Four |
| Five | Six | Seven | Eight |
| Nine | Ten | Eleven | Twelve |
| Thirteen | Fourteen | Fifteen | Sixteen |
| Seventeen | Eighteen | Nineteen | Twenty |

### 1.15

a Twenty   b Thirteen   c Five
d Seventeen   e Eight   f Sixteen

### 1.16

a  It's quarter to seven.
b  It's half past four.
c  It's five to ten.
d  It's quarter past two.
e  It's three o'clock
f  It's ten past three.

### 1.17

A  When do you start work?
B  At nine o'clock. What about you, what time do you start work?
A  At half past eight.
A  What time do you have lunch?
B  Um, at ten to one. And you, when do you have lunch?
A  Quarter past one.

### 1.18
a  I send 20 emails a day.
b  John has three meetings today.
c  They don't make any phone calls.
d  She doesn't receive 15 phone calls a day.

### 1.19
A  Hi, how are you?
B  Fine – busy, though. I have a lot of emails to read.
A  Really? How many emails do you receive?
B  Um, about fifteen a day. What about you, how many emails do you receive?
A  Around ten. What about phone calls, how many phone calls do you make?
B  About six a day. What about you?
A  Um, about eight. And how many phone calls do you receive?
B  Around four, but they're long. I spend a lot of time on the phone.

### 1.20
a  I make thirteen phone calls a day but my manager makes twenty.
b  I send three emails every morning but my manager sends fourteen.
c  I receive seventeen emails a day but I only send about two.
d  I have around fifteen meetings every week but my manager has nineteen.
e  I reply to eight emails in the morning and sixteen in the afternoon.
f  I have nine or ten phone calls to make every morning

### 1.21
a  Thirteen, Twenty
b  Three, Fourteen
c  Seventeen, Two
d  Fifteen, Nineteen
e  Eight, Sixteen
f  Nine, Ten

### 1.22
a  When do you start work?
b  What time do you have lunch?
c  How many phone calls do you receive a day?
d  When do you finish work?
e  When do you wake up?

### 1.23
I have a meeting at half past four.
I leave work at ten past five.
I make phone calls at half past six.
I start work at ten past eight.

## 03 WHERE DO YOU WORK?

### 1.24
A  Hello – do you like the conference?
B  Yes, it's great. New technology is very interesting.
A  Yes, it is. I'm Sofia Pereira.
B  Nice to meet you. I'm Daniel. Daniel Almeida.
A  Where are you from?
B  I'm from Sao Paulo.
A  Sao Paulo? Great, and where do you work?
B  I work for Appetizer. It's a food and drink company.
A  Sounds interesting. What do you do?
B  I'm a technician. I fix computers. And what about you? Where are you from?

### 1.25
**Conversation 1**
A  So, where do you work, Michael?
B  I work for Emirates Airlines, in Dubai.
A  Sounds interesting. What do you do, exactly?
B  I'm a receptionist. I answer the phone but I also do a lot of other things…

**Conversation 2**
A  Hi, I'm Fatma, good to meet you.
B  And you. I'm Sara.
A  What do you do, Sara?
B  I'm a human resources manager at El Corte Inglés.
A  El Corte…?
B  El Corte Inglés. It's a big retail company in Spain.
A  Okay. How big is it?
B  It's a very big company.
A  Really?
B  Yes, it's an interesting job. I organize company training sessions. Where do you work, Fatma? Is new technology important in your job?

### 1.26
A  Hello, I'm Estella.
B  Nice to meet you, Estella. I'm Carlo.
A  Good to meet you. Where do you work?
B  Well, I work in finance. I work for Acorn Bank.
A  Really? That's interesting. I'm in retail.
B  Okay. So what do you do?
A  I'm a human resources manager. I train staff. Technology is very important in my job.
B  I see. Where do you work?
A  I work for Corieza. My office is in Buenos Aires and I travel to different cities around Argentina.
B  How big is Corieza?
A  Enormous. It has about 5,000 stores worldwide.
B  5,000? That's a lot. And in Argentina?

### 1.27
a  10  20  30  40  50
    60  70  80  90  100
b  100  200  300  400  500
    600  700  800  900  1000
c  100  1,000  10,000
d  500  5,000  50,000

### 1.28
a  It costs 30 Euros.
b  The programme lasts 50 hours.
c  We have about 40 taxis.
d  We have 500 stores worldwide.
e  It has about 4,000 staff.
f  It has 100 employees.
g  It has 60,000 employees.
h  It has just 8 employees. It's very small.
i  40,000 people work there.
j  It has 1,000 employees in total.

### 1.29
A  Hi, I'm Bianca.
B  Hello, Bianca, good to meet you. I'm Freddie.
A  Nice to meet you, Freddie. So, where do you work?
B  I'm in the construction sector. I work for Dream Build.
A  Great! Tell me about Dream Build. How big is it?
B  Oh, well, it has about 2,500 staff in total.
A  2,500? That's big.
B  Yes, it's a big company, and it's a great company to work for.
A  And what do you do?
B  I work in sales. I sell our company's products all around the country.
A  So are you a sales manager?
B  Yes, that's right. I'm a sales manager.
A  Actually, so am I…

### 1.30
A  I'm Abdullah. Good to meet you.
B  Hello, I'm David. Nice to meet you. Where do you work?
A  I'm in tourism. I work for Gulf Air.
B  Okay, Gulf Air. How big is it? How many employees does it have?
A  Oh, about 3,000 I think.
B  I see. And what do you do?
A  I'm a flight attendant. I serve customers in first class.
B  Sounds interesting.
A  And you? Where do you work?

### 1.31
a  Hello, I'm Maya. I'm in tourism.
b  Nice to meet you. I'm Selma and I work in finance.
c  A  So, what do you do, Marion?
    B  Well, I work in the energy sector. I'm a gas engineer.
d  Great to meet you, Jacob. I'm Georgio and I work in construction.

### 1.32
Thirteen            Thirty
Three hundred       Three thousand
Seven               Seventy
Seventeen           One thousand seven hundred
Sixteen             Sixty
Six                 Six thousand

### 1.33
a  It's a small company. It has about 15 employees.
b  The company has offices in 17 countries.
c  The bank employs over 5,000 staff worldwide.
d  We have 12 taxis.
e  My company has a total of 700 employees.

# LISTENING SCRIPTS

## 04 CAN I HELP YOU?

### 1.34

A  Good morning, Parasol, how can I help you?
B  Good morning. Can I speak to Mr González please?
A  Okay. Can I ask who's calling?
B  It's Kristina Müller.
A  I'll just check if he's available.
A  I'm sorry. Mr González is not in the office today. Can I help you?
B  No, it's okay. When will Mr González be back?
A  Tomorrow. Can I take a message?
B  Yes please. Can he call Kristina Müller on zero one six four three two zero two six double four nine?
A  Okay, I'll just repeat that number. It's zero one six four three, two zero two, six double four nine. Is that right?
B  Yes, that's right.
A  Okay. Is there anything else?
B  No thank you, bye.
A  Goodbye.

### 1.35

a  Double zero double four / two oh eight / six four eight / seven double five nine
b  Plus four one / six zero eight / five eight seven / four four seven seven
c  Plus one two / double nine seven / five four one / double three two four
d  Double zero double eight / double eight seven / seven zero seven / six eight four one

### 1.36

A  Good morning, Purchasing.
B  Hello, can I speak to Kristina please?
A  This is Kristina Müller.
B  Hi, Kristina, it's José González here.
A  Oh, hi, José, how are you?
B  Good thanks, and you?
A  Good. Anyway, I want to talk to you about an order. Can we meet?
B  No problem, I'm free on Thursday morning.
A  Oh, I'm busy Thursday morning. What about the afternoon?
B  Oh, I can't meet in the afternoon. Friday?
A  I'm busy in the morning, Can we meet in the afternoon?
B  I'm free all afternoon. What time is best?
A  I can do 3.00 pm. Can we meet then?
B  Fine, I'll see you then.
A  Great, bye.
B  Bye.

### 1.37

Monday    Thursday    Saturday
Tuesday   Friday      Sunday
Wednesday

### 1.38

January, February, March, April, May, June, July, August, September, October, November, December

### 1.39

1  My birthday's on the 3rd of April.
2  I get my bonus on the 6th of November.
3  It's a public holiday on the 1st of January.
4  My wedding anniversary is on the 18th of August.
5  It's my birthday on the 22nd of February.

### 1.40

A  Good morning, international sales. How can I help you?
B  Hi, Kristina, It's José here. Thanks for your message.
A  Hi, José. Thanks for calling me back. Can I change the date for our next meeting?
B  Sure, that's no problem.
A  So, can we change the meeting from the 23rd of July to the 18th of August?
B  The 18th of August, I think that's okay. Let me check.
A  Sure, no problem.
B  Oh, I'm busy on the 18th. Can we meet on the 14th of August?
A  Let me check. Yes, the 14th is good.
B  Great, so see you on the 14th August.
A  See you then, bye.

### 1.41

Double oh two eight / double three four / double four five four
Double zero double two / two three four / double three double four
Double oh double five / double seven eight / eight double nine two
Double oh double four / two oh eight / four five six / double seven double four

### 1.42

a  Can we meet on Monday?
b  Sorry, I can't. I'm busy.
c  I can meet on Tuesday. Is that okay?
d  I can't meet in the morning. I have another meeting.
e  Can we meet in the afternoon?
f  I'm free then. We can meet on Tuesday afternoon.

### 1.43

Monday, Tuesday, Wednesday, Thursday, Friday, Saturday, Sunday

### 1.44

January, February, March, April, May, June, July, August, September, October, November, December

### 1.45

A  Good morning, how can I help you?
B  Hello, can I speak to Mr Smith, please?
A  Can I ask who's calling?
B  It's Samantha Lyons.
A  I'll just check.
A  I'm sorry, Mr Smith is out of the office today, can I take a message?
B  Can he call Samantha Lyons, please?
A  No problem. Is there anything else?
B  No thanks, bye.
A  Bye.

## 05 I'M HERE TO SEE JO

### 1.46

A  Good morning. Welcome to EuroClass Hotels head office.
B  Good morning. I'm Alex Kantar. I'm from EuroClass Paris. I'm here to see Jo.
A  Jo Schmitt?
B  Yes, Jo Schmitt, that's right.
A  Thank you. I'll just see if she's in her office. Just a moment, please.
A  Hello, Jo. Alex Kantar is here to see you. She'll be here in a moment. Please take a seat.
B  Thank you.

### 1.47

A  Hello, Alex, and welcome to Frankfurt. I'm Jo. Pleased to meet you.
B  Pleased to meet you, Jo.
A  So, Alex, how are you?
B  Very well, thanks. And you?
A  I'm fine, thanks. How was your journey?
B  It was very good, thanks. The train was on time.
A  Great. Are you new to EuroClass?
B  Yes, I am – I started last year.
A  Is this your first visit here?
B  Yes, it is. This is a great building.
A  Thank you. It's new. Can I get you a coffee?
B  Yes please, that would be great. Thank you.
A  So, how's business?
B  Good thanks.

### 1.48

A  Lovely coffee, thank you.
B  You're welcome. Let's have a look around.
A  Thank you.
B  First of all, the toilets are here, next to Reception.
A  Okay, thank you.
B  And there's a small kitchen for staff to use.
A  That's useful.
B  My office is also on this floor. Let me show you.
A  Thanks.
B  It's just through the main doors… Here we are. This is my office.
A  Oh, it's great.
B  And here's the main Administration office. This is Angela, our Department Administrator. Angela, this is Alex Kantar, the Marketing Assistant at EuroClass Paris.
C  Good to meet you, Alex. Welcome to EuroClass Frankfurt.
A  Thank you. Pleased to meet you.
B  Angela can help you with any problems. Just ask.
A  That's good, thank you.
B  And this is Ronald, our Head of Finance.
A  Pleased to meet you, Ronald.
B  Oh, and finally this is Roberta – she's Head of HR. The HR department is down the corridor. Do you have any questions?
A  Er, where's the boss?

### 1.49

There's a coffee area on the first floor next to meeting room 1. At the end of the first floor corridor there's a visitors' meeting room. Then, opposite the coffee area is meeting room 3. The marketing office is opposite meeting room 1.

### 1.50

a  I can meet in Paris.
b  When can we meet?
c  I'm here to see Jo.
d  How was your journey?
e  Is this your first visit here?
f  That would be lovely.
g  This is my office.

## 06 LET'S MAKE A START

### 2.01

A  So, thanks for coming everyone. I'm going to chair the meeting and Judy Foster is going to take the minutes. I'll just read the agenda. There are three items in total. The first item is the problem in Japan.
B  Sorry Carol, can I interrupt? Are problems in other countries also on the agenda?
A  Yes, we can do that at the end as the third item. The second item on the agenda is changes to laws in France.
C  So you mean we need to find solutions to the problems in France?
A  Yes. Okay, so let's go onto our first item, problems in Japan.

### 2.02

A  Right, I have another meeting. So many meetings!
B  Really, that many? How often do you have meetings?
A  Oh, it's not too bad, actually. Only sometimes, about twice a week. What about you?
B  I'm always in a meeting. We have meetings every day, actually. I'm writing the agenda for tomorrow now. Do you always read the agenda at the beginning?
A  Sometimes. We don't always use an agenda, but I always take the minutes, at every meeting. Do you take minutes?
B  No, I don't do that. I never take the minutes. I usually chair the meeting, about three or four times a week. How often do you chair meetings?
A  Oh, sometimes, probably about once a month. Anyway, sorry, I need to go, my other meeting's starting.

### 2.03

A  So, let's move onto the next item. Any comments?
B  Well, I think we should focus on Internet advertising. It's the future of advertising.
C  I understand, but many more people watch TV, so we should focus on TV advertising.
D  Could I jump in here? TV and Internet advertising are expensive, but not very effective.
A  That's a good point. What would you suggest?
D  Well, in my opinion, we should advertise in several types of media. A mixed advertising strategy.
B  I see what you mean.
C  Okay, but we need to reach the largest number of customers, that's TV and Internet. A mixed advertising strategy costs too much money and doesn't reach everyone.
A  Could I just say we need to decide on the advertising budget first, so maybe we should move onto that and then decide on the strategy?

### 2.04

a  How often do you read the agenda?
b  Do you always read the minutes?
c  Do you usually chair the meeting?
d  How often do you lead meetings?
e  How often do you have meetings?

## 07 BUSINESS ON THE MOVE

### 2.05

My first computer was expensive, and it was slow to start. I was happy with it, but I'm much happier with my new computer. Computers were slow then, and they were big, but today they are small and very fast. Today, I do a lot of my work on my tablet.

### 2.06

Simon Sinek is a writer and teacher in business and leadership. When he was young, he lived in London, South Africa and Hong Kong. Then he moved to the USA. He now lives in New York. He studied at City University in London, and now teaches business at Columbia University in New York. Simon Sinek introduced the idea of the 'golden circle'. This starts with the question 'Why?'. After that, it asks the question 'How?' and finally, it asks the question 'What?' This is the topic of his book – its title is *Start With Why*. He works in the USA, and gives talks and lectures. His talk on Ted.com is very popular, and millions of people watch it every year!

### 2.07

a  Simon Sinek is a writer and teacher in business and leadership.
b  He lived in London, South Africa and Hong Kong.
c  Then he moved to the USA.
d  He studied at City University in London.
e  Simon Sinek introduced the idea of the 'golden circle'.
f  This starts with the question 'Why?'.
g  After that, it asks the question 'How?'
h  He works in the USA.

### 2.08

lived, liked, wanted, moved, worked, started, asked, studied, showed, introduced

### 2.09

A  Hello everybody. Today we're talking to Peter Calabrini, who works in the Business department of HSBC. Thanks for coming in today, Peter.
B  You're welcome.
A  Right, just to make a start, tell us about yourself. Where did you live when you were young?
B  Well, when I was at school I lived in Liverpool, then we moved to Manchester.
A  What was your favourite subject at school?
B  Actually I really liked maths. I wanted to go into banking.
A  Really? Where did you go to university?
B  I studied mathematics at Leeds University.
A  Okay, and what did you do after that?
B  After that, I worked for the Bank of Scotland.
A  Uh-huh. What do you do now?
B  Now, I live in London and I work for HSBC.
A  I see, and do you enjoy your job …?

### 2.10

a  I studied at university.
b  She was a student at the Beijing Business School.
c  I work for Administrators Unlimited.
d  What did you do?

### 2.11

work – worked
start – started
show – showed
live – lived
want – wanted
like – liked
ask – asked
decide – decided
introduce – introduced

## 08 I'D LIKE TO TALK ABOUT…

### 2.12

Hi everyone. Today, I'd like to present the sales results for key regions and show changes from last year.

First, let me explain results for Europe. Sales decreased across Europe. They fell from $13 million to $9 million.

Now, I'll outline performance in North America. Sales in North America increased. They grew from $11 million to $13 million. This is because we launched new products in this market.

Finally, I'll talk about what happened in Asia. Sales also rose in Asia. They went up from $14m to $15 million.

So to recap, sales in the USA and Asia got better, but sales in Europe got worse.

# LISTENING SCRIPTS

## 2.13
a Today, I'd like to present the sales results for key regions.
b First, let me explain results for Europe.
c Now, I'll outline performance in North America.
d Finally, I'll talk about what happened in Asia.
e So, to recap, sales in the USA and Asia got better.

## 2.14
A Okay, so that's all from me. Does anyone have any questions?
B Yes, I have a question. Did investment go up in all countries?
A No, not in all countries, but it increased globally. Any other questions?
C I'd like to ask about investor confidence. Did investor confidence get worse?
A No, it got a lot better. People are happy about the global economy. Anyone else?
D Yes, what about government debt? Did the government debt rise?
A It's high, but it fell last month.

## 2.15
a Did profits fall last year?
b Profits increased last year.
c Did costs rise last month?
d Costs went down last month.
e Did sales go up last month?
f Sales went up last year.

## 09 WHERE SHOULD I STAY?

## 2.16
A You know, I think we should have a launch event for SE1 Training.
B You're right, we should. That's a great idea!
A Okay, let's plan it. What date is good?
B Well, it's August now, so after the summer holidays, in September.
A Good idea. September 10th?
B Hmm, that's early, maybe later in the month?
A Well, September 25th looks good. There's nothing in the diary.
B Okay then.
A Good, September 25th. And how long?
B Oh, I think three hours is about right.
A Three hours? No, I think that's too long.
B Okay, maybe you're right. Two hours then?
A Yes, two hours is good.
B Great. And for the venue you said a hotel is a good idea.
A Yes, we should go for one of the hotels in the centre of London.
B The Rex is nice.
A Erm, but it's expensive.
B I guess you're right. How about the Rialto?
A Whoa, that's expensive, too. I think the Regent is a great hotel, and it's cheap. You know, in Central Square.
B Yes, sure. You're right. Okay, let's book the Regent Hotel.
A Okay, good. When will we start?
B Oh, I think 6 is good.
A Hmm, what about 5?
B Well, I think 5 o'clock is too early – a lot of people are still at work then, so I think 6 pm is better.
A Yes, I see what you mean. Okay, let's go for 6.
B 6 pm it is then.
A Great. Well, we've got a time and a place. Now, what about food and drink?

## 2.17
A Hello, Dani's Catering Services. How can I help you?
B I need some food and drink for an event tomorrow.
A Tomorrow! But it's 5 pm now!
B I know, sorry. Our caterer has an emergency, so she can't do it!
A Oh dear. Well, what do you need?
B Do you have any chicken or fish?
A Erm, chicken, yes, but we don't have any fish.
B Okay, well, most people like chicken, don't they?
A Yes, but some people are vegetarian.
B That's true. Do you have any salad?
A Yes, but don't forget, salad can be difficult to eat.
B Yes, right. Okay, we won't have any salad.
A We have some very good pizza. Cheese and tomato – what about that?
B That sounds nice. Let's have some pizza. Vegetarian pizza, and chicken – great!
A Okay, fine. Do you want any dessert?
B Hmm, maybe not. We want a snack, not a complete meal.
A You could have some cake. Everyone likes cake.
B Yes, fine, cake is a good idea. Okay, that's the food. Now, what about drinks?

## 2.18
**Conversation 1**
A Great launch party!
B Yes, it is.
A I always like to make new contacts.
B Yes, so do I. Sorry, what's your name?
A Emma Mountford.
B Pleased to meet you, Emma. I'm Luis Sánchez.
A Great to meet you, Luis, is it your first visit here?
B To London? Yes, it is. Do you live here?
A Yes, I do. I'm from Cambridge, but I live in London now.
B Great. I only arrived here last night. Where should I go? What should I see?
A You should visit the city centre.
B Right.
A You can see lots of museums and galleries.
B Sounds good.
A And the shopping is great.
B Okay, where should I go?
A You should go to Oxford Street. Or Regent Street, near here.
B Excellent. Thanks for …

**Conversation 2**
A Hello, are you enjoying the party?
B Yes, it's good. How about you?
A Well, yes, it's great. So many people.
B I know!
A I'm Tarkan.
B It's good to meet you, Tarkan. I'm Sophie.
A Nice to meet you, Sophie. Are you from London?
B Yes, I am. And you?
A I'm from Istanbul, in Turkey.
B Ah.
A Do you know it?
B No, but I hope to go there next year for a conference.
A Really? Well, it's a very beautiful city. You'll like it.
B What should I see there?
A Well, you could go to the bazaar, in the old city centre. It's great for shopping, better than the shopping centres.
B That sounds nice.
A Yes, and in Istanbul you can find a lot of old buildings, but also modern hotels and shops.
B Uh-huh, wonderful. Is there anything else I should do?
A Well, yes, lots of things, like …

## 2.19
a Beach
b Hotel
c Shop
d City centre
e Museum
f Art gallery
g Stadium
h Park

## 2.20
a I like salad.
b I don't like chicken.
c I like pizza, but I don't like sandwiches.

## 10 IS CASH OK?

### 2.21

**A** Okay, that's agreed. Can we talk about price now?
**B** Sure, what do you want to talk about?
**A** Well, we'd like a ten per cent discount.
**B** Sorry, but that's difficult. We only give a five per cent discount.
**A** That's okay, we'll take five per cent. Could we pay in 120 days?
**B** I'm afraid that's too long for us, what about 90 days?
**A** Okay, we'll take 90 days. Is bank transfer okay?
**B** That's fine.
**A** Great. So, we'll pay in 90 days, by bank transfer, with a five per cent discount, right?
**B** That's right.

### 2.22

**A** Okay, so let's talk about the delivery and then we can write the contract.
**B** Okay.
**A** Will you organize delivery?
**B** Yes, we will.
**A** What company will you use?
**B** We'll use Tailor's, they're very good.
**A** That's fine. Will you pay all the delivery costs?
**B** Sorry, but we won't pay all the delivery costs. We agreed that we will pay 50% each.
**A** Oh, yes, that's right. I forgot. Okay, we'll pay 50% each. And will you deliver on Thursday the 19th of May?
**B** Yes, we will, in the morning. I'll phone you to confirm.
**A** Great. Right, shall we write the contract?
**B** Great.

### 2.23

**a** Could we pay in 90 days?
**b** 90 days is a bit difficult.
**c** That's okay.
**d** I'm afraid we need a bank transfer.
**e** Is cash okay?

Macmillan Education
The Macmillan Building, 4 Crinan Street, London N1 9XW
A division of Macmillan Publishers Limited
Companies and representatives throughout the world

ISBN 978-0-230-45879-6

Text © Edward de Chazal and Ed Pegg 2015
Design and illustration © Macmillan Publishers Limited 2015

The authors have asserted their rights to be identified as the authors of this work in accordance with the Copyright, Designs and Patents Act 1988.

First published 2015

All rights reserved; no part of this publication may be reproduced, stored in a retrieval system, transmitted in any form, or by any means, electronic, mechanical, photocopying, recording, or otherwise, without the prior written permission of the publishers.

Designed by emc design Limited
Illustrated by Matthew Hams pp42, 44, 62; Dave Russell pp16, 38
Cover design by emc design Limited
Cover photograph by Getty Images/E+
Picture research by Susannah Jayes

Authors' acknowledgements:

Edward de Chazal
I would like to thank and acknowledge the excellent support of my co-author, Ed Pegg and the publishing and editorial team at Macmillan. Many thanks too, to my family for their patience.

Ed Pegg
This book was built on cups of tea and I'd like to thank Monia for making them for me. I'd also like to thank my co-author, Edward de Chazal, and the fantastic editorial team at Macmillan for all their work and ideas.

The publishers would like to thank the following people, schools and institutions for their help in developing *In Company 3.0* Starter level: Brian Brennan, International House, Barcelona; Matt Carmody, Linguarama Ibérica, Barcelona; Matthias Fuchs, Siemens AG, Germany; Louise Hankey, British Council, Barcelona; Tina Kagemann, Munich Volkshochschule, Munich; Sean O'Malley, Interlang, Madrid; Matilde Seara, EOI Jesús Maestro, Madrid; Elain Skarsten-Pflieger, Learning Circle, Augsburg; Jenny Smedley, Ziggurat English Services, Barcelona; Ian Stride, John Carry, Robert Davies, Michael Delahunty, Lester Drake, Dilys Kevan and John Milne, International House, Madrid.

Special thanks to Dr. Stefan Fodor, arenalingua, Germany; Noeleen Bufler, Augsburg Volkshochschule, Augsburg; and Sarita Simmons, Very Good English Language Training, Munich, Germany for all their invaluable contributions, suggestions and advice.

Many thanks also to all the teachers around the world who took the time to complete our *In Company* online questionnaire and who have contributed to the development of the *In Company* series.

The authors and publishers would like to thank the following for permission to reproduce their photographs:
**Alamy**/alt.PIX Pte Ltd p37, Alamy/AST Fotoworks p30(bcl), Alamy/Paul Bock p64, Alamy/Cultura Creative (RF) p22(a,f), Alamy/Li Ding p24(A), Alamy/Kevin George p20(f), Alamy/Golden Pixels LLC p17, Alamy/imageBROKER pp24(F),70(tr), Alamy/INTERFOTO pp51(tcl), Alamy/Izel Photography p70(c), Alamy/Patti McConville p67(d), Alamy/moodboard p70(bl), Alamy/numb p20(e), Alamy/Paul Rapson p70(b), Alamy/kristian sekulic p8, Alamy/Stock-miester p22(b), Alamy/Martin Thomas Photography p20(bl), Alamy/Urbanmyth p66(bcm), Alamy/Bartosz Wardziak p22(d); **Corbis**/Jon Feingersh/Blend Images p71, Corbis/KidStock/Blend Images p28, Corbis/Andrew Brookes p70(a), Corbis/H. Armstrong Roberts/ClassicStock p51(tl), Corbis/ Ghislain & Marie David de Lossy/cultura p72, Corbis/Philippe Body/Hemis p67(c), Corbis/Hero Images p29, Corbis/Image Source p22(e), Corbis/237/Paul Bradbury/Ocean p43, Corbis/68/Ciaran Griffin/Ocean p22(tr), Corbis/Eric Audras/Onoky p22(c), Corbis/Alan Schein Photography p25, Corbis/Jonathan Ross/Spaces Images p67(e), Corbis/the food passionates p20(d), Corbis/Topic Photo Agency p66(cmr); **Getty Images**/AFP p67(b), Getty Images/Robert Churchill p56, Getty Images/Caiaimage/Sam Edwards p44, Getty Images/elkor p23(cl), Getty Images/Fuse pp58–59, Getty Images/Alexander W Helin p30(bcr), Getty Images/JupiterImages p23(cr), Getty Images/Sean Justice p66(cr), Getty Images/Günay Mutlu p24(B), Getty Images/Johnnie Pakington p66(cm), Getty Images/Photo by Philippe Petit/Paris Match via Getty Images p51(bcl), Getty Images/peepo p53(cl), Getty Images/Tetra Images p10(tr); **Glow Images**/Hemant Mehta p16; **MACMILLAN NEW ZEALAND** p24(E); **Simon Sinek**/https://www.startwithwhy.com p52; **Superstock**/age fotostock/age footstock p36; **Thinkstock**/AAA !aAAAAA p65(H), Thinkstock/aizram18 p65(A), Thinkstock/Anson_iStock p30(br), Thinkstock/Bobboz p50(d), Thinkstock/carlosbezz p67(f), Thinkstock/claudiodivizia p48(cmr), Thinkstock/daboost p50(a), Thinkstock/denitzachtereva p76(d), Thinkstock/Digital Vision p9, Thinkstock/draghicich p76(b), Thinkstock/Givaga p51(bl), Thinkstock/Joe Gough p76(a), Thinkstock/Ciaran Griffin p50(f), Thinkstock/Hemera Technologies p48(cl), Thinkstock/koosen p48(cr), Thinkstock/lucadp p50(b), Thinkstock/Oleksiy Mark p50(e), Thinkstock/Gabrielle Morehead p65(B), Thinkstock/ninikas p76(c), Thinkstock/Zoonar/N. Okhitin p66(br), Thinkstock/Stephen Orsillo p20(h), Thinkstock/Sergej Petrakov p65(f), Thinkstock/pilipphoto p65(C), Thinkstock/mercedes rancaAo p67(a), Thinkstock/rez-art p76(f), Thinkstock/Scott Rothstein p24(d), Thinkstock/scanrail p50(c), Thinkstock/Hellen Sergeyeva p24(C), Thinkstock/Shailth p65(E), Thinkstock/slava296 p66(bmr), Thinkstock/Slavica Stajlic p65(D), Thinkstock/Maksim Toome p65(G), Thinkstock/UmbertoPantalone p48(cml), Thinkstock/underworld111 p30(bl), Thinkstock/Wavebreakmedia Ltd p53(tl), Thinkstock/Wittybear p20(g), Thinkstock/XiXinXing p10(tmr), Thinkstock/Yellow Dog Productions p53(tcl), Thinkstock/zeleno p76(e); **Toshiba** p54(cl,cml).

Commissioned photographs by Nick Miners pp 20, 21, 34, 35, 48, 49, 62, 63, 76, 77.

These materials may contain links for third party websites. We have no control over, and are not responsible for, the contents of such third party websites. Please use care when accessing them.

Printed and bound in Thailand
2019  2018  2017  2016  2015
10  9  8  7  6  5  4  3  2  1